Hazard

The Extinction Protocol guide to risk mitigation

Hazard

By Alvin Conway

ISBN: 978-1-105-82444-9

Lulu Publishing
860 Aviation Parkway
Suite 300
Morrisville, NC 27560
(919) 459-5858

Contents

Acknowledgements

God, the source of life and love in the universe, beautiful

Family - All TEP readers, Ellivahpla – much love

The recommendations contained herein are not meant to
supersede the advice or counsel of professional authorities.

Introduction

"God has put within our lives, meanings and possibilities that quite outrun the limits of mortality." –Harry Emerson Fosdick

Our planet is one of continuous change and dynamism. Sometimes this change can be disruptive to cycles of life on our planet, and sometimes this evolving dynamism increases risk factors, which threaten the safety and well-being of the Earth's diverse population. These risks are global and without borders, prejudice, or nationality. The current geology of our planet is experiencing transitional shifts of change, which we occasionally refer to as earthchanges. These geological changes increase climatic, environmental, seismic, and volcanic risk factors for the planet's population at large. Change is not merely confined to the geophysical world. Change is also occurring in the geopolitical and social spheres of our planet. The planet's population is dramatically increasing, border disputes among nations with burgeoning populations are increasing, economic stability is eroding as sovereign debts mount, nation states are disintegrating from political turmoil, pandemic disease threats are increasing, conflicts are proliferating, and natural resources are becoming scarce and more expensive to both extract and transport. All of these sweeping changes enhance risk factors, which can imperil the security and safety of everyone living on the planet. What are some of these risks?

- Number of nuclear weapons on the planet – 23,000

- Number of nuclear reactors in the world – 440

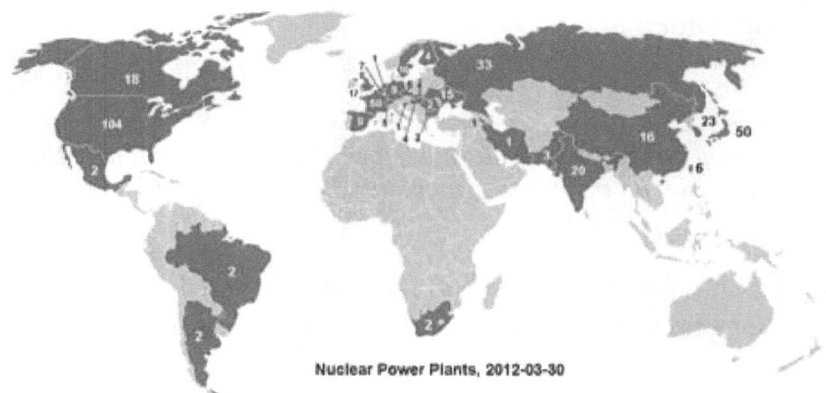

Nuclear Power Plants, 2012-03-30

- Number of nations with ICBM nuclear missiles – 9

- Number of nations with chemical weapons program – 26

- Number of nations with biological weapons programs – 19

- Number of active volcanoes in the world – 1500

- Number of earthquakes that occur in the world annually – 2 million

- Number of people living in high-risks seismic zones – 500 million

This is not a survival book; it's a survivor's book. This book is about the planet's many hazards and risk factors and how, in many cases, those hazard risks can be mitigated. What is essential to our continual survival and well-being, as a species, is a thorough understanding of the geology, ecology, and the inherent risks posed by natural and man-made threats on our planet. This book has made an attempt to index some of these most serious hazards.

Manufactured – Biological – Chemical – Pathogen

Nuclear or chemical weapons

"No weapon that is formed against thee shall prosper; and every tongue that shall rise against thee in judgment, thou shalt condemn. This is the heritage of the servants of the Lord, and the righteousness is of me, saith the Lord." –Isaiah 54:17

Nuclear Threat – war, terrorism, and nuclear plant meltdown

This is the most dangerous of all man-made hazards other than bioterrorism. Understanding this hazard is essential for your survival. Ionized radiation is radiation composed of particles that individually can liberate an electron from an atom or molecule, producing ions, which are atoms or molecules with a net electric charge. These tend to be especially chemically reactive, and that reactivity produces the highest biological damage caused, per unit of energy of ionizing radiation. There are various types of ionized radiation. These include: ionizing radiation produced by radioactive decay, nuclear fission and nuclear fusion, and by particle accelerators and naturally occurring cosmic rays.

Nuclear war

"Today, every inhabitant of this planet must contemplate the day when this planet may no longer be habitable. Every man, woman and child lives under a nuclear sword of Damocles, hanging by the slenderest of threads, capable of being cut at any moment by accident, or miscalculation, or by madness. The weapons of war must be abolished before they abolish us." –U.S. President John F. Kennedy in an address before the General Assembly of the United Nations on September 25, 1961.

The threat of nuclear war hangs over the planet, as John F. Kennedy says, like the sword of Damocles. Geopolitical tension in the world, global economic sovereign debt defaults, conflict over natural resources, nuclear proliferation and terrorism, could all be catalysts for a thermonuclear war. A nuclear attack could happen anywhere in the world from a country or rogue states. An attack by a nation would likely be preceded by a deteriorating political situation. A war with conventional weapons, between nations that possess nuclear weapons, if not ended swiftly, could also morph into a nuclear conflict. Even limited nuclear strikes in one region of the world carry the likelihood of initiating an all-out nuclear war elsewhere.

An unconventional nuclear attack by terrorists or rogue states could come without warning. It may come in the form of a dirty bomb or improvised nuclear explosive device. Given the lack of a credible sovereign enemy, such attacks are very unlikely to escalate to a full nuclear exchange.

When nuclear war is imminent in a country like the United States, it will go to a DEFCON status. DEFCON is a defense readiness condition and alert posture used by the United States Armed Forces. The DEFCON system was developed by the U.S. Joint Chiefs of Staff to unify and specify combatant commands. The defense protocol prescribes five graduated levels of readiness (or states of alert) for the U.S. military, and the increase in severity from DEFCON 5 (least severe) to DEFCON 1 (most severe) is used to match varying military scenarios.

- DEFCON 5. Normal peacetime readiness

- DEFCON 4. Normal increased readiness, increased intelligence and national security measures. (Cold War.)

- DEFCON 3. Increased force readiness above normal, American radio call signs are changed to classified call signs. Air Force ready to mobilize in less than 15min.

- DEFCON 2. Increase in force readiness, just below maximum. All forces ready to mobilize and deploy within 6 hrs. (Declared only once during the Cuban Missile Crisis.)

- DEFCON 1. Maximum force readiness; the use of nuclear weapons has been authorized. This has never been used for the national condition though, at times, certain military units were placed at DEFCON 1, for certain conflicts.

There are several types of nuclear or radiological bombs you should also be familiar with. These include:

- SDD – Simple Dispersal Device
- RDD – Radiological Dispersal Device
- NRS – Nuclear Reactor Sabotage
- IND – Improvised Nuclear Device
- NW – Nuclear Weapon

There are also different types of nuclear payloads, or bombs that could be delivered by missile from; an airplane, mobile launch vehicle, submarine, land-based ICBM (Intercontinental Ballistic Missile), artillery shell, parked car, drone, low orbit satellite, launch vehicle, or land-based device. These include:

- Fission atomic bombs are the most basic nuclear weapon. Their explosive yield is derived from splitting heavy nuclei (plutonium and uranium) with neutrons. As the uranium or plutonium split, each atom releases great amounts of energy, and more neutrons. The daughter neutrons cause an extremely fast nuclear chain reaction. Fission bombs have been the only type of nuclear bomb used in war so far. Two were dropped on Japanese cities during World War II. The development of fusion bombs has almost relegated the 'straight fission' bomb to history. All nuclear capable nations are now thought to also be in possession of fusion bombs.

- Fusion H-Bombs, which are also known as hydrogen bombs, use the incredible heat of a fission bomb 'spark plug', to compress and heat deuterium and tritium (isotopes of hydrogen), which fuse and release immense amounts of energy. Fusion weapons are also known as thermonuclear weapons, since high temperatures are required to fuse deuterium and tritium together. Such weapons are usually many times more powerful than the bombs that destroyed Nagasaki and Hiroshima in World War II. Most nuclear tests conducted by industrialized nations in the 1950s and 1960s were thermonuclear bomb tests.

- EMP Weapons: A nuclear weapon detonated at a very high altitude can generate an electromagnetic pulse so powerful; it can destroy electronic and electrical devices. There are also bombs designed to create EMP blast effects that can be used in missiles, or launched from airplanes, submarines, or drones. Placing radios and flashlights in a sealed metal container, known as a Faraday cage, will protect sensitive electronics from EMP blast effects, provided the items being protected are not in contact with the enclosure. The metal shield must surround the protected item completely - and it helps if it is grounded.

- A Neutron bomb or enhanced radiation weapon (ERW), or weapon of reinforced radiation is a type of thermonuclear weapon designed specifically to release a large portion of its energy as energetic neutron radiation (fast neutrons), rather than explosive energy. Although their extreme blast and heat effects are not entirely eliminated, it is the enormous radiation released by ERWs that is meant to be a major source of casualties. The levels of neutron radiation released are able to penetrate thick, protective materials such as armor, making them useful anti-tank weapons.

- A Thermobaric weapon, which includes the type known as a *"fuel-air bomb,"* is an explosive weapon that produces a blast wave of a significantly longer duration than those produced by condensed explosives. Most thermobaric weapons are non-nuclear. The bombs work on detonation basically by sucking the oxygen out of the air. This is useful in military applications where its longer duration increases the numbers of casualties and causes more damage to structures. There are many different variants of thermobaric weapons, including rounds that can be fitted to hand held launchers, such as RPGs and anti-tank weapons.

The Defense

TEP

HAZARD THREAT

In the event of a nuclear attack, you must act quickly to ensure your survival. If you are not at home or near a fallout shelter (which shields one from radiation fallout), you must have the necessary skill set to survive such a disaster. If it is an explosive bomb attack, particularly a dirty bomb, you can expect localized and downwind contamination from the explosion, and the dispersion of radioactive materials. If you are close enough to see or hear any local bomb blast, assume that it includes radiological or chemical agents. You should immediately move away from the blast area as quickly as possible. If the wind happens to be blowing toward you from the blast direction; travel in a direction that is crosswise or perpendicular to the wind, as you move away from the blast area. If possible, cover your face with a dust mask or cloth to avoid inhaling potentially radioactive dust. Upon reaching a safe secured location, remove your outer clothing outside, and shower as soon as possible. Tune into news sources for the latest updated information, and for additional instructions about sheltering or potential evacuation. Remember, local government and emergency hazmat officials are better prepared than you, to direct and assist the public in 'dirty and chemical bomb' emergencies.

Seek shelter immediately. Aside from the geopolitical warning signs, your first warnings of an imminent nuclear attack will most likely be an alarm or warning signal that could come from your local Civil Defense Agency; if not, the warning may be from the blast itself. A nuclear detonation is both a horrific and compelling sight; however, *the seconds spent gawking at the sight could mean the difference between life and death.* The bright light from the detonation of a nuclear weapon can be seen ten miles away from ground zero. If you are within the vicinity of the blast radius, or what's known as ground zero, your chances of survival are virtually nonexistent, unless you happen to be in a shelter or underground bunker that provides adequate protection from both the blast and the radioactive fallout. If you are a few miles out, you will have about 10-15 seconds until the heat wave hits you, and maybe 20-30 seconds until the shock wave does. *Under no circumstances, should you look directly* *at the fireball.* On a clear day, this can cause temporary blindness even at very long distances. Many of the victims of both the Hiroshima and Nagasaki atomic bombs in World War II had their eyes burned out of their sockets from staring at the fireball. The actual damage radius is highly variable. It depends on the size of the bomb detonated, the altitude of the explosion, and even the weather conditions present at the time of the blast.

The after effects of an atomic blast are horrific, so getting out of an open environment is critical for your survival. If you can't find shelter, seek a depressed area of ground like a ditch or ravine nearby and lay face down, exposing the least amount of skin as possible. If there is no shelter of this kind, dig as fast as possible and create a make-shift trench. Even at around 8 kilometers (5 miles) from the blast, you will suffer third degree thermal burns; and at 32 kilometers (20 miles), the heat can still burn the skin off your body. The wind itself will peak at around 960 kilometers per hour (600 mph), and will level anything or anybody caught in the open. Seeking adequate shelter is critical for survival.

Quick urban emergency shelters:

- Underground parking garage, lowest floor
- Basement or bank vault
- Bunker or storm drain
- Mausoleum or concrete crypt
- Subway
- Concrete pipe

Provided none of the above shelters are readily available, get indoors immediately and retreat to the innermost room of the house or building, away from windows, patios, or balconies. This will offer some protection from the heat and radiation of the initial blast wave. Avoid windows and stay away from glass. The blast waves from an atomic bomb will shatter windows, even if you are miles from the blast epicenter. If you are in Switzerland or Finland, radiation shelters should be plentiful throughout the country. Know where they are and plan exit routes prior to any emergency.

Types and half life of radioactive material

- Iodine -131 is 8 days
- Strontium -90 is 29.1 years
- Cesium -137 is 30 years
- Plutonium -244 is 80 million years
- Uranium -235 is 700 million years
- Uranium -236 is 2 billion years

Alpha particles are the weakest, and during an attack, are virtually non-existent as a threat. Alpha particles will remain suspended inches in the air for a few hours before they are absorbed by the atmosphere. They possess a minuscule threat however, in that they could be fatal if ingested or inhaled. Standard clothing will generally help protect you from Alpha particles.

Beta particles are faster than Alpha particles and can penetrate matter. They will travel for up to 10 meters (10 yards) before they are absorbed into the atmosphere. Exposure to beta particles carries high risks. One may develop *"Beta burns,"* which mimic sunburn. Beta particles are able to penetrate living matter to a certain extent and can change the structure of impacted molecules. In most cases, such change can be considered hazardous, with damage possibly as severe as cancer and death. If the struck molecule is DNA, it can exhibit signs of spontaneous mutation.

Gamma rays are the deadliest type of known radiant electromagnetic emission. Gamma rays have the smallest wavelengths, and carry the most energy of any wave in the electromagnetic spectrum. Gamma rays can traverse nearly a mile in the air, and penetrate just about any kind of shielding. Gamma radiation can also cause severe damage to the internal organs. Sufficient shielding will be required. Gamma rays and neutrons harbor many dangers including: causing diffuse damage throughout the body, prompting radiation sickness, cell DNA damage, cell death, and increased incidence of cancer rather than burns. This fact is reflected in data showing cancer rates increased by more than 32% for survivors of the atomic bombs dropped on Japan in WWII.

Preparation for domestic shelters should begin even before the perceived threat of a thermonuclear attack. Take any such threats mentioned in the news very seriously, because local government officials certainly do. It may also be essential to know that during any such emergency; local, federal, and military officials will have their hands full and will also be exploring retaliatory measures, as they were for the U.S. 9-11 disaster. Do not expect immediate help, and be prepared to sustain your own existence for at least 8 days if necessary. Begin reinforcing your make-shift shelter from the inside by stacking dirt around the walls or lining it with anything else you can find. If you are in a trench, do your best to enclose it with a roof, but only if materials are nearby; don't expose yourself to a 'hot environment' any more than you have to. It is impossible, at a very fundamental physical level; to completely shield yourself from all radiation- what you are doing is really mitigating risks. Use the following to help you determine the amount of material you'll need to reduce radiation penetration to 1/1000:

- Steel: 21 cm (0.7 feet)
- Rock: 70-100 cm (2-3 ft)
- Concrete: 66 cm (2.2 ft)
- Wood: 2.6 m (8.8 ft)
- Soil: 1 m (3.3 ft)
- Ice: 2 m (6.6 ft)
- Snow: 6 m (20-22 ft)

Radiation sickness

Absorbed doses of radiation are measured in a unit called a gray (Gy). Diagnostic tests that use radiation, such as an X-ray, result in a small dose of radiation — typically well below 0.1 Gy, focused on a few organs or small amount of tissue. Signs and symptoms of radiation sickness usually appear when the entire body receives an absorbed dose of at least 1 Gy. Doses greater than 6 Gy to the whole body are generally not treatable, and usually lead to death within two days to two weeks, depending on the dose and duration of the radiation exposure.

Initial signs and symptoms

Acute radiation syndrome: The initial signs and symptoms of treatable radiation sickness are usually nausea, vomiting, and headaches. The amount of time between exposures and when these symptoms develop, is an indicator of how much radiation a person has absorbed. After the first round of signs and symptoms, a person with radiation sickness may have a brief period with no apparent illness, followed by the onset of new, more serious symptoms. In general, the greater your radiation exposure, the more rapid and more severe your symptoms will be. Severe symptoms could show up after a week. These include: diarrhea, nausea, vomiting, fever, hair loss, disorientation, weakness, and low blood pressure.

Iodine treatment

"Stable iodine is an important chemical needed by the body to make thyroid hormones. Following a radiological or nuclear event, radioactive iodine may be released into the air and then breathed into the lungs of any being breathing that air. Radioactive iodine may also contaminate the local food supply and get into the body through food or drink. In the case of internal contamination with radioactive iodine, the thyroid gland quickly absorbs this chemical. Radioactive iodine absorbed by the thyroid can then injure the gland. Because non-radioactive iodine acts to block radioactive iodine from being taken into the thyroid gland, it can help protect this gland from injury." [1]

Treatment for radiation poisoning

Potassium Iodide is available at very reasonable prices via Amazon. For additional information on quantities, check: Source Naturals Potassium Iodide 32.5mg, 240 tablets.

Potassium Iodide (KI) Information

Taking potassium iodide (KI) tablets after an incident involving radioactive materials may or may not limit the risk of damage to a person's thyroid gland from ionizing radiation. The Centers for Disease Control and Prevention (CDC) has prepared some information to further explain when KI might be appropriate and what people should consider before making a decision to take KI.

When to take KI?

Local emergency management officials will tell people when to take KI. If a nuclear incident occurs, officials will have to find out which radioactive substances are present before recommending that people take KI. If radioactive iodine is not present, then taking KI will not protect people. If radioactive iodine is present, then taking KI will help protect a person's thyroid gland from the radioactive iodine. Taking KI will not protect people from other radioactive substances that may be present along with the radioactive iodine. The Food and Drug Administration (FDA) recommends that KI be taken, as soon as the radioactive cloud containing iodine from the explosion is close by. KI may still have some protective effect, even if it is taken 3 to 4 hours after exposure to radioactive iodine. Because the radioactive iodine will be present in the initial blast and decays quickly, a single dose of KI may be all that is required.

The FDA recommendations on KI can be reviewed online by browsing *FDA guidelines on KI.*

Forms of KI, and how much should be taken

KI comes in tablets of 130 mg. A one time dose at the levels recommended is usually all that is required. However, if a person expects to be exposed to radioactive iodine for more than 24 hours, another dose should be taken every 24 hours.

People should listen to emergency management officials for recommendations after an incident. According to the FDA:

- Adults should take one 130 mg tablet.
- Children between 3 and 18 years of age should take one-half of a 130 mg tablet (65 mg).
- Children between 1 month and 3 years of age should take one-fourth of a 130 mg tablet (32 mg).
- Infants from birth to 1 month of age should be given one-eighth of a 130 mg tablet (16 mg)
- Women who are breastfeeding should take the adult dose, and their infants should receive the recommended infant dose.
- Children who are approaching adult size (greater than or equal to 150 pounds) should take the adult dose regardless of their age.

KI tablets can be stored for at least 5 years without losing their potency. People should remember that taking a higher dose of KI, or taking KI more often than recommended, will not offer more protection, and could cause severe illness and death, due to allergic reaction.

How might a nuclear incident cause thyroid damage? There are some types of radioactive incidents which release radioactive iodine. The thyroid gland, which will use any iodine that is in a person's bloodstream, cannot tell the difference between radioactive and non-radioactive forms of iodine. Because of this, the thyroid would rapidly absorb radioactive iodine just as it does iodine from a person's diet. The radioactive iodine releases energy (radiation) that, in high concentrations, can damage the cells of the thyroid gland. In some people, especially young children, this damage can cause thyroid cancer or other diseases of the thyroid within a few years of the exposure. What is potassium iodine? It is one of several ingredients that can be added to table salt to make it iodized. KI has also been approved by the FDA as a nonprescription drug for use as a "blocking agent" to prevent the human thyroid gland from absorbing radioactive iodine. However, KI may not provide people with 100% protection against all radioactive iodine. Its effectiveness will depend on a variety of factors, including when a person takes it, how much iodine is already in the person's thyroid, how fast the person's body processes it, and the amount of radioactive iodine the person is exposed to. Iodized table salt will not provide enough iodine to protect the thyroid and should not be used as a substitute.

Why would KI be important in the event of a nuclear incident?

Because the thyroid will rapidly absorb any iodine that is in the body, people may need to take KI tablets soon after an incident that involves radioactive iodine. The KI will saturate the thyroid gland with iodine and help prevent it from absorbing radioactive iodine. However, KI does not prevent the effects of other radioactive elements. Using KI will only protect the thyroid gland from radioactive iodine. It will not protect other parts of the body from radioactive iodine, and it will not protect a person from other radioactive materials that may be released.

Who should or should not take KI when the public is told to do so?

Children are the most susceptible to the dangerous effects of radioactive iodine. The FDA and the World Health Organization (WHO) recommend that children from newborn to 18 years of age all take KI unless they have a known allergy to iodine.

Women who are breastfeeding should also take KI, according to the FDA and WHO, to protect both themselves and their breast milk. However, breastfeeding infants should still be given the recommended dosage of KI to protect them from any radioactive iodine that they may breathe in or drink in breast milk.

Young adults between the ages of 18 and 40 have a smaller chance of developing thyroid cancer or thyroid disease from exposure to radioactive iodine than do children. However, the FDA and WHO still recommend that people ages 18 to 40 take the recommended dose of KI. This includes pregnant and breast-feeding women, who should take the same dose as other young adults.

Adults over the age of 40 have the smallest chance of developing thyroid cancer or thyroid disease after an exposure to radioactive iodine, but they have a greater chance of having an allergic reaction to the high dose of iodine in KI. Because of this, they are not recommended to take KI unless a very large dose of radioactive iodine is expected. People should listen to emergency management officials for recommendations after an incident.

Medical conditions that make it dangerous to take KI

The high concentration of iodine in KI can be harmful to some people. People should not take KI if they:

- Have ever had thyroid disease (such as hyperthyroidism, thyroid nodules, or goiter).

- Know they are allergic to iodine (as in x-ray dye or shellfish).
- Have certain skin disorders (such as dermatitis herpetiformis or urticaria vasculitis).
- Consult with your doctor prior to an emergency to see if the ingestion of KI will cause potential health complications for you.

The thyroid is a small gland located in a person's neck on either side of the breathing tube (trachea). The thyroid has two parts, a right lobe and a left lobe, that are connected by a small strip of tissue called the isthmus. The main function of the thyroid gland is to create, store, and release thyroid hormones. These hormones regulate the body's metabolism. Why is iodine important to the thyroid gland? The thyroid gland takes iodine from the bloodstream and uses it to make thyroid hormones. Without the required amounts of iodine, the thyroid will not be able to make these hormones. Most of the iodine in people's bodies comes from the food they eat. [2]

Nuclear power plants

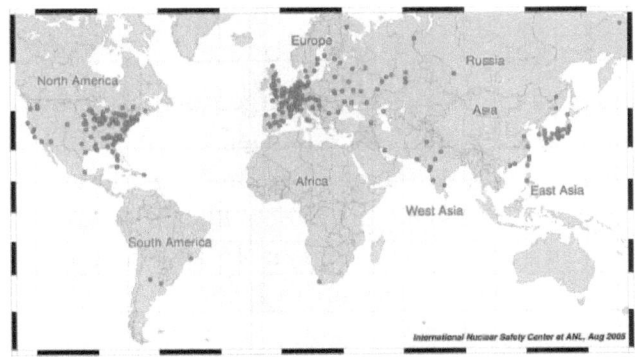

Nuclear power plants located throughout the world

Nuclear Plant locations United States

U.S. nuclear power reactors

Of the 104 nuclear power reactors in the U.S., 23 are the same design as the Japanese reactors hit by the earthquake and tsunami. Where the Mark 1 boiling water reactors are located:

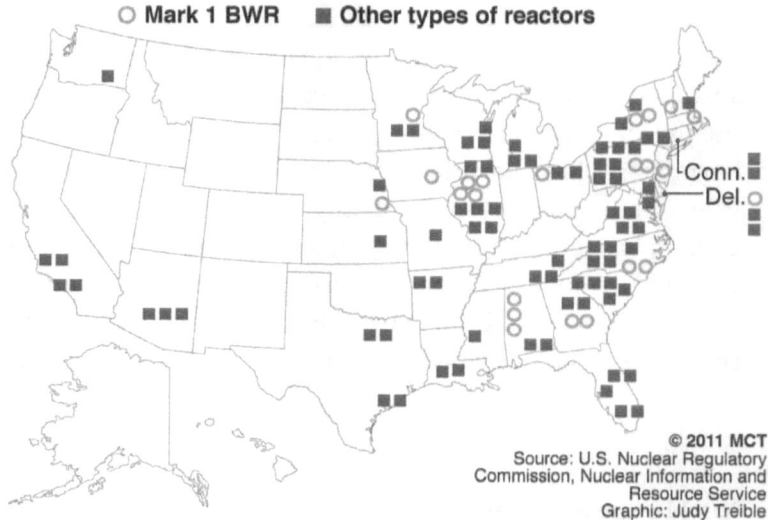

○ **Mark 1 BWR**   ■ **Other types of reactors**

© 2011 MCT
Source: U.S. Nuclear Regulatory
Commission, Nuclear Information and
Resource Service
Graphic: Judy Treible

Nations with nuclear reactors: Argentina 2, Armenia 1, Beligum 7, Brazil 2, Bulgaria 2, Canada 18, China 16, Czech Republic 6, Finland 4, France 58, Germany 9, Hungary 4, India 20, Iran 1, Japan 53, Korea Republic 23, Mexico 2, Netherlands 1, Pakistan 3, Romania 2, Russian Republic 33, Slovakian Republic 4, South Africa 2, Spain 8, Sweden 10, Switzerland 5, Taiwan 6, Ukraine 15, United Kingdom 17, United States 104.

Biological Attack

Biological weapons and the use of bio-terror is one of the greatest terrorist threats facing society today. A biological attack is the deliberate release of germs or other biological agents designed to infect or contaminate a populace. Some of these agents must be inhaled, enter through a cut in the skin, or be ingested to make you sick. Some biological agents, such as anthrax spores are not contagious. Anthrax kills the person who inhales the spores. Agents like the smallpox virus, can result in a contagious outbreak, which can induce an epidemic or pandemic.

Unlike an explosion, a biological attack may or may not be immediately obvious. The mode of delivery can be silent, and that's what makes this threat so sinister and dangerous. While it is possible that you will see signs of a biological attack, as was the case with the anthrax mailings in the U.S, it is perhaps more likely that local health care workers will first report a pattern of unusual illness or there will be a wave of sick people suddenly seeking emergency medical attention. This is known as a cluster outbreak. It is a red flag.

You will learn about the incident through the news or an emergency radio or TV broadcast, or some other signal used in your community. If the crisis is serious enough, it will prompt emergency broadcast civil defense warnings. Emergency response workers may be dispatched to warn residents in a neighborhood if there is a need to enact quarantine measures. In the event of a biological attack, public health officials may not immediately be able to provide information on what you should do. Information could be scarce, and may be released to the public in trickles, due to national security concerns. It will take time to determine the nature of the illness, its specified hot zone, its mode of transmission, how it should be treated, and who is at immediate risk from the attack. However, you should watch TV, listen to the radio, or check the Internet for official news to gather facts about the following:

- Are you in a suspected hot zone?
- What are the signs and symptoms of the disease?
- Are medications or vaccines being administered?
- Is an evacuation or quarantine required?
- Who should get the vaccinations or seek immediate medical treatment?
- Where have facilities been designated for emergency medical care if you become sick?

Protect yourself

If you become aware of an unusual and suspicious release of an unknown dangerous substance nearby, your first response should be to protect yourself. Establish a safe distance, and report the incident to the appropriate authorities. Be especially cautious if the substance emits a foul odor. In which case, cover your mouth and nose with layers of fabric that can filter the air, but still allow breathing; or use an emergency mask from a smaller emergency kit, which you have secured in your car or at work. Examples for make-shift masks include: two to three layers of cotton, such as a t-shirt, handkerchief, or towel. Otherwise, several layers of tissue or paper towels may help. Wash off with soap and water, and contact authorities as soon as you are in a safe environment. If you suspect you have been contaminated; avoid all contact with other people, and confine yourself to a restricted area.

Watch for symptoms and use good hygiene

At the time of a declared biological emergency, look for symptoms which may indicate illness. Anthrax infections can manifest symptom from one to five days. The incubation period for smallpox is 7 to 14 days. Use common sense; practice good hygiene and cleanliness to avoid spreading germs to others, and seek medical advice if the situation warrants.

Responding to an attack

Aside from their common lethality, various chemical or biological agents require different responses. Familiarize yourself with them. Chemical agents are generally liquids, often aerosolized, and most have immediate effects, or are delayed for a few hours. Anthrax can be administered in a powdered form. Many chemical agents have a unique odor and color. Biological agents differ in that the effects are delayed, often for days. The effects of toxins, such as botulism toxin, occur typically in less than a day. Live biological agents, such as anthrax or a plague, generally take 2-5 days for symptoms to appear. Biological agents have no odor or color and can be administered in either liquid or powder form. There are many different potential chemical and biological agents that a terrorist could use as a weapon, but we can make the following broad generalizations:

- Although food or water contamination or absorption through the skin are potential attack routes, most experts agree that inhalation of chemical or biological agents is the most likely and effective means of transmissibility.

- Protection of breathing airways is therefore the single most important factor in a situation, where chemical or biological agents may be present. Many likely agents are heavier than air and would tend to stay close to the ground. In those cases, this dictates an upward safe-haven strategy away from potentially lethal inhalations.

Basic decontamination procedures

The Defense

TEP

HAZARD THREAT

Thorough scrubbing with large amounts of warm soapy water or a mixture of 10 parts water to 1 part bleach (10:1) will greatly reduce the possibility of absorbing an agent through the skin. If water is not available, talcum powder or flour are also excellent means of decontamination of liquid agents. Sprinkle the flour or powder liberally over the affected skin area, wait 30 seconds, and brush it off with a rag or gauze pad. Try to avoid abrasions on the skin. (Note: *the powder absorbs the agent so it must be brushed off thoroughly*. If available, rubber gloves should be used when carrying out this procedure.) Generally, chemical agents tend to present an immediately noticeable effect, whereas many biological agents will take days before symptoms appear. In either case, medical attention should be sought immediately, even if exposure is thought to be limited. Most chemical and biological agents, that pose an inhalation hazard, will break down fairly rapidly when exposed to the sun, diluted with water, or will dissipate in high winds. This offers a safety margin, provided you utilize it to dispossess yourself of potential contamination threats. No matter what the agent is or its concentration, evacuation from the area of attack is always advisable, unless you are properly equipped with an appropriate breathing device and protective clothing, or have access to collective protection. Vinegar or milk provides some effective relief of diluting contaminates in pepper spray or tear gas.

Warning signs of an attack or incident

A chemical or biological attack or incident won't always be immediately apparent, given the fact that many agents are odorless and colorless, and some cause no immediately noticeable effects or symptoms. Be alert to the possible presence of agents or radical changes in the environment. Here are some potential indicators to watch for that might signify an attack:

- Droplets of oily film on surfaces
- Unusual dead or dying animals in the area
- Unusual liquid sprays or vapors
- Unexplained odors (smell of bitter almonds, peach kernels, newly mown hay or green grass)
- Unusual or unauthorized spraying in the area
- Victims displaying symptoms of nausea, difficulty breathing, convulsions, disorientation, or patterns of illness inconsistent with natural disease.
- Low-lying clouds or fog unrelated to weather; clouds of dust; or suspended, possibly colored, particles.
- People dressed unusually (long-sleeved shirts or overcoats in the summertime) or wearing breathing protection, particularly in areas where large numbers of people tend to congregate, such as movie theaters, subways, high-rises, or stadiums.

What to do in an attack

Protection of breathing airways is the single most important thing a person can do in the event of a chemical or biological incident or attack. You may not be able to fully assess the dangers of the situation, until after the area has been heavily contaminated, and people start manifesting symptoms of illness. Prepare to evacuate and mitigate risks by following proper safety protocols. While evacuating the area, cover your mouth and nose with a handkerchief, coat sleeve, or any piece of cloth to provide some moderate means of protection. Other basic steps one can take to avoid or mitigate exposure to chemical or biological agents include:

- Stay alert for attack warning signs. Early detection enhances survival.
- Always move upwind from the source of the attack.
- If evacuation from the immediate area is impossible, move indoors (if outside) and upward to an interior room on a higher floor. Remember many agents are heavier than air and will tend to stay close to the ground. If the attack occurs in a multi-story building, seek the safest and quickest exit possible.
- Once indoors, close all windows and exterior doors, and shut down air conditioning or heating systems to prevent circulation of air. If you are driving through a suspected contaminated area, *never turn on the air-conditioning system in your vehicle.*
- Cover your mouth and nose. If gas masks are not available, use a surgical mask or a handkerchief. An improvised mask can be made by soaking a clean cloth in a solution of 1 tablespoon of baking soda in a cup of water. While this is not highly effective, it may provide some temporary protection until you can get to safety.
- Cover exposed arms and legs where possible, and make sure any cuts or abrasions are properly covered or bandaged.

- If splashed with an agent, immediately wash it off using copious amounts of warm soapy water or a diluted 10:1 bleach solution. Properly dispose of your clothing in a plastic, air-tight bag.
- If you are in a car, shut off outside air intake vents and roll up the windows if no gas has entered the vehicle. Late model cars may provide some protection from toxic agents. In any case of suspected exposure to chemical or biological agents, medical assistance should be sought as soon as possible, even if no symptoms are immediately evident.
- Seek medical attention and consult hazmat emergency personnel as soon as possible.

Standard decontamination procedures

COMPARISON DATA DECONTAMINATION LEVELS/TECHNIQUES				
LEVEL	TECHNIQUE	BEST START TIME	DONE BY	GAINS
Immediate	Skin decontamination	Before 1 minute	Individual	Stop agent from pene-trating.
	Personal wipedown Operator's spraydown	Within 15 minutes	Individual or crew	
Operational	MOPP gear exchange	Within 6 hours	Unit	Possible temporary relief from MOPP 4. Limit liquid agent spread.
	Vehicle washdown		Battalion, crew, or decon platoon(-)	
Thorough	Detailed equipment/ aircraft decon	When mission allows reconsti-tution	Decon platoon	Probable long-term MOPP reduc-tion with min-imum risk.
	Detailed troop decon		Unit	

Notes:
1. The techniques become increasingly less effective the longer they are delayed.
2. Performance degradation and risk assessment need to be considered when exceeding 6 hours. See FM 3-4, BDO risk assessment.
3. Vehicle washdown is most effective if started within 1 hour, but will often have to be delayed for logistical reasons.

Pestilence

"He that dwelleth in the secret place of the most High shall abide under the shadow of the Almighty. I will say of the LORD, He is my refuge and my fortress: my God; in Him will I trust. Surely He shall deliver thee from the snare of the fowler, and from the noisome pestilence. He shall cover thee with his feathers, and under his wings shalt thou trust: his truth shall be thy shield and buckler. Thou shalt not be afraid for the terror by night; nor for the arrow that flieth by day; nor for the pestilence that walketh in darkness; nor for the destruction that wasteth at noonday. A thousand shall fall at thy side, and ten thousand at thy right hand; but it shall not come nigh thee. Only with thine eyes shalt thou behold and see the reward of the wicked. Because thou hast made the LORD, which is my refuge, even the most High, thy habitation; there shall no evil befall thee, neither shall any plague come nigh thy dwelling. For he shall give his angels charge over thee, to keep thee in all thy ways. They shall bear thee up in their hands, lest thou dash thy foot against a stone." -Psalm 91:1-12

Preparation for a pandemic

A pandemic is an epidemic of infectious disease that has spread through human populations across a large region; for instance, multiple continents, or even worldwide. The Spanish Flu outbreak of 1918 would be considered an example of a pandemic. For epidemiologists, this is the worst scenario imaginable- a pandemic of disease, in an escalating outbreak, to which the human populace has no natural immunity. A widespread endemic disease that is stable, in terms of how many people are getting sick from it, is not a pandemic. Further, flu pandemics generally exclude recurrences of seasonal flu. Throughout history there have been a number of pandemics, such as smallpox and tuberculosis. More recent pandemics include the HIV pandemic and the H1N1 pandemic of 2009-2010. Here are some of the incubation periods for some very dangerous communicable and zoonotic (animal to human) diseases:

Incubation periods

- Cholera – 4 to 12 hours, death in 18 to 48 hours if untreated
- Smallpox – 7 to 17 days
- Dysentery – 1 to 4 days
- Malaria – 10 to 28 days
- H Series Influenza – 1 to 4 days
- Whooping Cough (Pertussis) – 7 tc 10 days
- Tuberculosis – 2 to 12 weeks
- Ecoli infection – 3 to 8 days
- Salmonella – 12 to 72 hours

Depending on the threat level, some diseases will require immediate medical attention, or antibiotic treatment; others will require full quarantine. Smallpox would be the most serious of these threats. If there is a fatal outbreak of any pathogen that is causing cluster illness or deaths, it needs to be reported to health officials immediately. Remember, quarantine is due to a biological event, and not a chemical or nuclear incident. In a state of emergency, health authorities may ask you to place a sign outside your door if you are exhibiting symptoms from a dangerous outbreak. Epidemiologists do this to create a radius map of the outbreak, so they can pinpoint its cause and point of origin. A proper quarantine will protect you from various chemical and biological threat scenarios; henceforth, we will cover different aspects of quarantine procedures.

A new disease can always come out of nowhere. Microbes are in a constant state of evolution, and antibiotic resistance is growing world-wide. Ecoli, salmonella, C diff infections, tuberculosis, and cholera are all getting harder to treat with traditional antimicrobials, so there is always a chance for an outbreak of super-strains from previously known diseases. Should a pandemic of any kind break out, the World Health Organization (WHO), the Centers for Disease Control and Prevention (CDC), and other governmental and non-governmental organizations will provide: information on the spread of the disease, updates on vaccines or other prescribed medications, health and safety tips, and travel advisories. Do not expect the information to come quickly. Generally, it is a slow process where fear typically trumps facts, especially in the case of a large number of fatalities. It is therefore highly advisable that you conduct your homework before an outbreak occurs. Travel restrictions and quarantines can also apply, so always be prepared in the event of an outbreak if you are ever stranded overseas during a vacation or while on business travel.

Influenza outbreaks since the 20ᵗʰ Century

- H1N1 – Spanish Flu, 1918
- H2N2 – Asian Flu, 1957
- H3N2 – Hong Kong Flu, 1968
- H1N1 – Swine Flu in U.S., 1976
- H1N1 – Russian Flu, 1977 (cause unknown)
- H1N1 – Swine Flu, Netherlands, 1986
- H1N1 – Swine Flu, Wisconsin, U.S., 1988
- H1N1 – Swine Flu, Netherlands, 1993
- H7N7 – Duck Virus, UK 1995
- H5N1 – Avian Flu, Hong Kong 1997
- H3N8 – Equine Influenza EI, Australia 2007
- H1N1 – Novel Influenza A, Mexico 2009
- H7N3 – Subtype Influenza, Mexico 2012

Influenza antiviral

The Defense

HAZARD THREAT

Two antiviral medications, Tamiflu and Relenza, have shown the potential to effectively prevent and treat avian flu. In the event of a severe influenza pandemic involving high fatalities, these medicines would be very difficult to obtain. A national declared state of emergency would likely restrict their use to medical facilities and emergency administrative health-care agencies. Tamiflu and Relenza are both available, only by prescription, and will probably be effective, only if taken before an infection or very shortly afterward. It should be noted that additional testing is necessary to determine how effective these drugs really are against a specified avian flu strain. Such information should be made available by health organizations, like the WHO and the CDC, but it could take some time before full testing is assessed on the drugs' effectiveness. Furthermore, mutations in the avian flu virus may render them ineffective over time.

Quarantine

The first and most basic stage of quarantine is to go home and to restrict your accessibility to the public. Emergency kits should not be used until needed, as the situation may grow progressively worse with the epidemic over time. Have someone you know drop off supplies or food in a box near your residence if possible. Do not seal off your home, as this procedure is used only for chemical events where you need to be indoors for a very short period of time. Most quarantines will last days, if not weeks or months. At this stage, you can actually go out in your front yard or back yard and breathe the air just fine, as long as you do not breathe someone else's air that might be infected with an airborne agent, communicable disease, or virus.

Be aware of your safety and health parameters. If you are concerned about contracting an infection after an outbreak, and you have to be in public, wear a surgical mask. All infected people should remain a good distance (minimum 20 feet) away from you, and anyone else sheltering with you. Anyone (again, including certain animals and some insects) that has been in a possibly infected area should be kept separate (quarantined separate) from you until they have sought proper medical attention (if it is available), been cleared, or they have run the course of the incubation period and remain asymptomatic. *Do not attempt to move or bury any animal suspected of being a host for an illness or disease-particularly rats or mice.* Keep in mind, most symptoms don't manifest until after the incubation period, which could last for several days.

In the event of a bio-terror attack, the latency period for some pathogens could be up to 2 weeks. If the pathogen is especially virulent, death could come within 72 hours of the first symptoms. If the pathogen is especially virulent, like a suspected smallpox outbreak, emergency health-care officials or military bio-terror soldiers will be deployed in biological containment suits. Usually at this stage, a gas mask with a biological filter is needed instead of a simple N-95 dust mask. Expect mass vaccinations from health providers in biological containment suits. In the case of smallpox or something of equal lethality, vaccinations will be mandatory by law. Be aware of official warnings, as to when events could escalate to this level.

Family or group plan of action

- Have a family emergency plan. When the pandemic starts; activate your plan. Make sure every family member knows what to do, when to report in, and proper quarantine procedures if they are caught in a hot zone. A *hot zone* is a region of lethality.
- If you are still on the road and/or in public, pull out your gas mask, with bio-filter, from the kit in auto.
- Keep the radio tuned to local stations you trust for local updates and information. Do not be alarmed by any news you cannot verify. Panic will be the order of the day during such incidents.

- Upon arriving home, start quarantine process by bringing everyone inside, including pets.
- Put a *"Quarantine"* sign on front door to ward off unannounced visitations, and to limit the risks of transmissibility.
- Start the bio-filtration system in your house, if you have one. Air filtrations machines will be especially helpful in filtering the air, but they will not contain or stop the spread of an infection.
- If possible, set up a decontamination station in your garage with drapes, shower, gloves, masks, and gowns. There are benefits to having an inclined drive in your garage. Draining hazardous water from a decontamination shower is the best example of that.
- Set up isolation rooms for possible sick family members and guests. These rooms should probably be located off of major traffic routes, like upstairs or at the far end of the house, so uninfected family members will have minimal exposure, as they traverse to and fro.
- Start everyone on immune system boosters as soon as possible, and make sure everyone gets their proper amount of sleep. A rundown body has no defense against infection. If you have to rotate in sleep shifts; do so.
- Check all electrical (solar, 12 volt, and battery) systems in case of a loss of power.
- Check water supplies and have everyone shower daily until there is a loss of water pressure.
- Check on the possibility of working from home.
- Put in requests by phone for advance homework assignments for school-age children to be sent over the Internet.

- Check with contacts you trust for updates on the situation, and avoid panic.

Atmospheric forces of nature – Tornado – Cyclone – Lightning – Blizzard

Tornado and hurricane

"For thou hast been a strength to the poor, a strength to the needy in his distress, a refuge from the whirlwind, a shadow from the heat, when the blast of the terrible ones is as a storm against the wall." -Isaiah 25:4

Tornado – the rage of wind

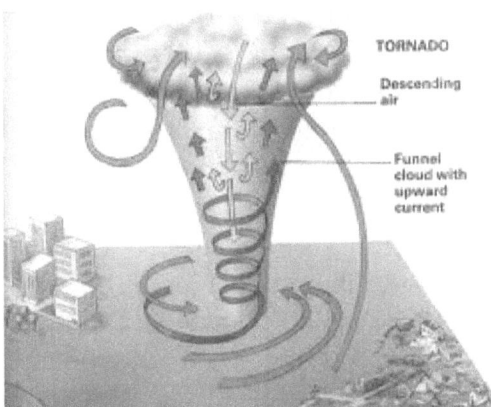

A tornado is a narrow, violent, rotating column of air that extends from the base of a thunderstorm to the ground. As the planet warms more, the atmosphere will become more unsettled and turbulent. Consequently, strong tornado storm systems will increase in frequency across the globe. Tornadoes are the most violent of all atmospheric storms. A visible sign of the tornado (a condensation funnel made up of water droplets), sometimes forms and may or may not touch the ground during the tornado's lifecycle. Dust and debris in the rotating column makes a tornado visible and confirms its presence. Most tornadoes have wind speeds less than 110 miles per hour (177 km/h), are about 250 feet (76 m) across, and travel a few miles (several kilometers) before dissipating. The most powerful tornadoes can attain wind speeds of more than 300 miles per hour (483 km/h), stretch more than two miles (3.2 km) across, and stay on the ground for dozens of miles (more than 100 km in some instances). The United States averages about 1,200 tornadoes per year. The greatest density cluster of tornadoes in the U.S. occurs in what's known as Tornado Alley. Tornado Alley is a section of the central U.S. Midwest. About 90% of tornadoes that erupt in Tornado Alley are spawned by the collision when cold, dry air from Canada and the Rocky Mountains meets warm, moist air from the Gulf of Mexico and hot, dry air from the Sonoran Desert. This phenomenon produces atmospheric instability, heavy precipitation, and many very intense thunderstorms. There are two types of tornadoes: those that come from a supercell thunderstorm, and those that are spawned independently. Tornadoes that form from a super-cell thunderstorm are the most common, and often the most dangerous. A supercell is a long-lived (greater than 1 hour), and highly organized storm feeding off an updraft (a rising current of air) that is tilted and rotating. This rotating updraft (as large as 10 miles in diameter, and up to 50,000 feet tall), can be present, as much as 20 to 60 minutes before a tornado forms. [1]

Tornado frequency around the world varies. The Netherlands is said to have the highest average number of recorded tornadoes per area of any country (more than 20, or 0.0013 per sq mi [0.00048 per km2], annually), followed by the UK (around 33, or 0.00035 per sq mi [0.00013 per km2], per year), but most of the tornadoes reported are small and cause only minor damage. In absolute number of events, ignoring area, the UK experiences more tornado outbreaks than any other European country, excluding waterspouts.

Tornadoes kill an average of 179 people per year in Bangladesh, the most in the world. The high fatality rate in Bangladesh is due to high population density, the poor quality of construction of buildings, and the lack of tornado safety knowledge among the country's populace. Other areas of the world that have frequent tornadoes include: South Africa, parts of Argentina, Paraguay, southern Brazil, as well as portions of Europe, Australia, New Zealand, far eastern

Asia, including China, the Philippines, and Japan. The intensity of a tornado is based on wind speeds calculated by something called the Enhanced Fujita or EF scale. An EF 5 storm is the most dangerous type of tornado. According to statistical data from the NOAA, since 1950, there have been 57 confirmed tornadoes rated F5 (EF5) in the United States and one in Canada and the numbers appear to be increasing. From 1999 to 2007, there were none reported in the U.S. and in 2008, there was only one. However, in 2011, there were a total of six EF5 tornadoes reported in the U.S., including the deadly EF5 tornado which struck Joplin, Mo on May 22, 2011 which killed 158 people and destroyed 75% of the town.

The EF tornado scale

OPERATIONAL EF SCALE	
EF Number	3 Second Gust (mph)
0	65-85
1	86-110
2	111-135
3	136-165
4	166-200
5	Over 200

Even with major advances in tornado prediction and tracking, you seldom have much time to prepare when a tornado actually strikes or when warning sirens are sounded. Weather is becoming more mercurial, as we mentioned, and thunderstorms can develop very quickly. Planning ahead, is the most important strategy you can implement to improve your chances of surviving a brush with a tornado.

The Defense

TEP

Hazard Threat

Move to a shelter. Watch the news service for reports of threatening weather. At the first sign of a tornado, or if a tornado warning has been issued, stop whatever you're doing and seek appropriate shelter immediately, even if you don't see a tornado. Seconds count, and could make the difference between life and death if a tornado is moving into your area. An underground tornado shelter or a specially designed tornado safe room is the safest place to be during a tornado. A basement, subway, or underground parking garages are all excellent safe places to retire to, in the event of a possible tornado. Many homes, businesses, and schools in areas prone to tornadoes already have safe retreat shelters- learn where they are prior to a tornado outbreak. If you live in a high-risk area, consider building a tornado shelter or buying a prefabricated shelter. The Federal Emergency Management Agency (FEMA) has produced a guide to building a shelter which you can access through their website.

Stay away from windows, and cover yourself with a mattress, cushions, or sleeping bags. If possible, get under a heavy table, which can protect you from falling debris. Make sure there is no space between you and floor, so you won't be lifted by the suction of air, in case the roof of your house is blown off by the tornado. If you are in a multi-story building, retire to the lowest floor, and seek the safety of a basement or hallway that is away from windows and mirrors. Do not use elevators. If the power goes out, you could be stranded between floors. Make sure all offices or rooms are closed in the hallway where you retire; and never stand behind a door to a room when a tornado is striking. Make note of where very heavy objects are on the floor above you, and avoid the area beneath these, as they could fall through a collapsing floor. If you have a one story house, retire to inner hall closet or take shelter in the innermost bathroom by laying face down in a bathtub, and covering yourself with a mattress or sleeping bag.

If you are in a vehicle and a tornado is very near you, get out of the car and seek shelter, as soon as possible, in the closest building. Park your car at the side of the road, out of traffic lanes. Cars are not safe shelters, and as tornadoes can travel at more than 60 mph, you should not take the risk of attempting to outrun it. Besides, the windows can be blown out from the atmospheric pressure differential of an approaching tornado. If the tornado is far away and you aren't near a good shelter, your best option--if traffic allows-- is to attempt to drive to shelter or at least out of the path of the storm. Look for parking garages in a mall, apartment complex, or sporting venue. Pick a stationary object near you and watch how the tornado moves relative to that object. If the tornado is moving to your left, you should drive to your right if possible; and if it's headed to your right, drive to your left. If the tornado does not appear to be moving either right or left, it's either moving directly away from you or, if it appears to be getting bigger or closer to you, right at you. If it's moving at you, leave your car and seek safety as instructed. Do not remain in open space under any circumstance. If you are near an overpass on an open highway, drive to a concrete overpass and park some distance from it. Take shelter in the understructure crevice incline.

Watch: A tornado watch means that there is a threat of tornadoes within the region specified, and that you should keep an eye on the news for the latest severe weather updates. A tornado watch can accompany a severe thunderstorm warning when there are clouds capable of producing rotation that can eventually turn into a meso-cyclone and then a tornado.

Warning: Tornado warnings mean that a sign of rotation has been detected on Doppler radar, and that you should take immediate action depending on the tornado's location, and its predicted (usually right) track or direction.

Emergency kit items

- Flashlight – hand cranked
- Batteries
- Battery powered radio
- Self Powered Radio
- Self Powered Flashlight
- Glow sticks (Candles may ignite gas)
- Emergency or hazard signs
- Clean clothes
- First-aid kit
- 5-10 gallons of water
- Non-perishable foods
- Rubber sole shoes in case of downed power lines
- Utility numbers
- Tools to turn off a ruptured gas line

After the tornado threat has passed; have a designated meeting place for everyone to check in. Assess the damage if any, and be prepared to call emergency or utility officials to report any incidents such as injuries, ruptured gas lines, or power outages. You will also need the phone and policy number of your insurance agent.

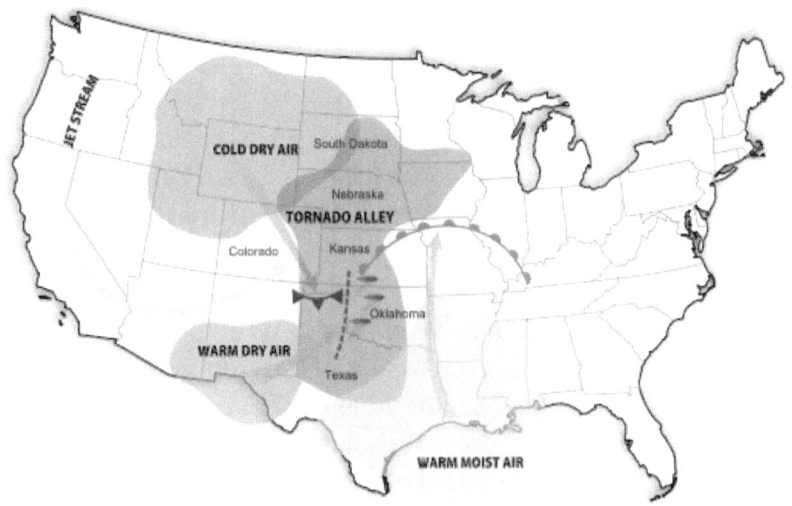

Tornado Alley of the U.S. and where and how tornadoes form. Credit NOAA

According to data compiled by the National Climatic Data Center for the period between January 1950 and July 2009, these U.S. states are ranked by the number of tornado outbreaks.

1. Texas: 8,049
2. Kansas: 3,809
3. Oklahoma: 3,442
4. Florida: 3,032
5. Nebraska: 2,595
6. Iowa: 2,368
7. Illinois: 2,207
8. Missouri: 2,119
9. Mississippi: 1,972
10. Alabama: 1,844

Cyclones – storms over the water

If you live near, or happen to be visiting: the Caribbean, the East coast of the U.S., the southeastern tropical rim of Asia, Central America, Australia, East Asia, NE Canada, Nova Scotia, Newfoundland, the Middle East Gulf, the South Pacific, northern Europe or Mexico, you should be aware of the threat posed by cyclones, typhoons, or tropical storms. Cyclonic force winds may be encountered all over the globe, but it is only above the warm seas of the tropics that a ripple of instability in the air can become a genuine cyclone; the deepest of all low-pressure weather systems. A cyclone is an area of closed, circular, fluid motion, rotating in the same direction as the Earth. This is usually characterized by inward spiraling winds that rotate counterclockwise in the Northern Hemisphere and clockwise in the Southern Hemisphere of the Earth. A *"tropical cyclone"* is a synonym for a hurricane. Most large-scale cyclonic circulations are centered on areas of low atmospheric pressure. The largest low-pressure systems are cold-core polar cyclones, and extratropical cyclones, which lie on the synoptic scale. Warm-core cyclones such as tropical cyclones, mesocyclones, and polar lows, lie within the smaller mesoscale. Cyclones begin in tropical regions, such as northern Australia, South-East Asia, and many Pacific islands. Cyclones sometimes drift into the temperate coastal areas, threatening more heavily populated regions to the South. Northern Australia has about four or five tropical cyclones every year during the summertime wet season. For a cyclone to develop, the sea surface must have a temperature of at least 26ºC.

Hurricane season (usually lasting from June 1 through November 30 in the United States) can be a nerve-racking time for everyone. Each season the West and Central Pacific region experiences 31 typhoons on average, about half of which have the potential to cause severe destruction. If you are traveling abroad during typhoon season, it is always a good idea to get travel insurance that will allow you to change your flight departure date, in the event of an unexpected emergency.

Typhoon and Cyclone Seasons – map NASA

- Hurricane U.S. and northern hemisphere: June 1 to November 30
- West North Pacific Basin: January to December
- Western South Pacific Basin: July of present year to June of following year

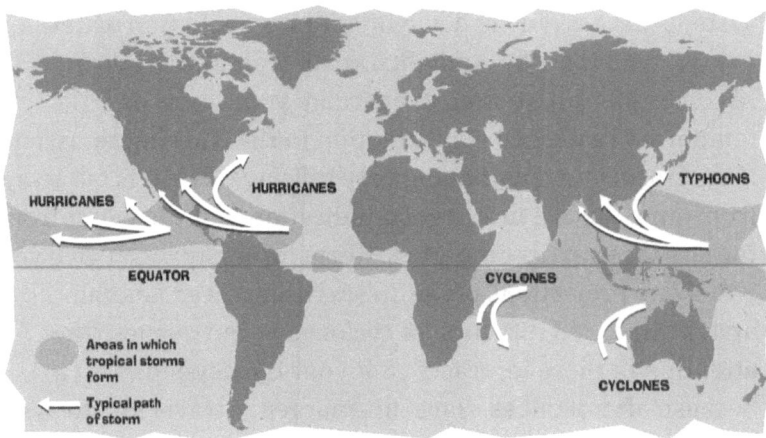

The following map gives you a wonderful view of where cyclonic storm systems form over the world's ocean basins. The arrows indicate the general movements of cyclones and hurricanes, in respect to adjacent continents and landmasses.

Be prepared for potential cyclones if you reside in the high-risk regions during storm season.

SAFFIR-SIMPSON HURRICANE SCALE

Hurricanes and cyclones can intensify quickly, often with very dangerous results. Most of the strengthening of cyclonic systems occurs during daylight hours, when ocean waters are warmed most by sunlight. Do not wait until a storm becomes life-threatening to evacuate your home or temporary residence. Pay attention to the warning signs, and if the storm is strengthening very quickly while it is far away from land, that's a pretty good indication that the worst from the storm is yet to come. Most storm forecasters can give you 3 to 4 day projections of the strength, expected landfall arrival time, and direction of cyclones or hurricanes. Pay attention to these forecasts, as if your life depended on it, because often; it does. Have an emergency travel kit always prepared for such emergencies to take with you in the event of an evacuation notice. If you are traveling, you should pack with the necessary items you need or be prepared to obtain them locally when you arrive at your destination. Hurricane intensity is based on the Saffir-Simpson hurricane scale, which goes from one to five depending on the speed and wind velocity of the storm.

The Defense

HAZARD THREAT

Strategy: Authorities suggest you should always have what they call a *'take box'* in your home that you could readily pick up and take with you in the likelihood that your house is ever threatened by fire, cyclone, earthquake, tornado, or any other natural disaster. The take box should have everything you need to reconstruct your life in the event you evacuate and everything is lost. Passports; birth, wedding, adoption, divorce, and armed service separation certificates; copies of insurance policies; mortgage information; house and car title. If you have a scanner, save yourself space and heartbreak by scanning family albums and images of other keepsakes, burn those to CD and keep a copy in your take box, or make a copy of all your pictures, videos, music and documents on an external hard drive that you can keep in your take box.

- Board up the windows of your house, in the event of an approaching storm, and make sure the gas is turned off before you leave.
- Cut trees or stray limbs that could fall on personal property in the likelihood of a storm. This may seem trite, but it could literally save you thousands of dollars in property damage from the winds of a vicious storm, if trees or limbs crashed into property.
- Have an emergency generator on hand in the event the power is disrupted in your neighborhood, which almost always happens when a major hurricane or cyclone comes ashore.

- Evacuate from low-lying areas that are deemed flood-prone. In December of 2011, Typhoon Washi killed 1,268 people in the Philippines, and most of the fatalities were the result of drowning, as similarly was the case with Hurricane Katrina in 2005. Katrina was the sixth strongest hurricane ever recorded, and the third strongest hurricane to ever make landfall in the U.S. More than 80% of the area of New Orleans was underwater; some places, by as much as 20 feet. The storm killed 1,836 people and caused $75 billion dollars in property damage. Despite the many warnings about the approaching danger of the storm, and the numerous government calls for evacuation, many people died needlessly because they never took the storm seriously. Katrina still ranks as one of the most costly disasters in U.S. history.
- Never drive through a badly flooded area in a car. It's virtually suicide.
- Have enough cash on hand to get through an emergency, and buy supplies in case ATMs or banks are inoperable or closed from power failure.
- Have an emergency kit ready for yourself and family members.
- Fulfill any languishing prescriptions before the onset of a major storm. If you are confined to an evacuation shelter for an extended period, a lack of much needed medicine could create inconsolable hardships.
- Cook anything you have in your freezer and then refreeze it. The idea is, if the power goes out, you can eat it first, when it thaws, and save your non-perishable food items for last.
- Have supplies of fresh drinking water on hand. In an emergency, a hot water heater can hold 50 to 75

gallons of fresh water. Tap the supply only if you need it.

- Have a bicycle for transport in case gasoline is unavailable, or your car is damaged.

Lightning

Lightning is a gigantic electrostatic discharge (the same kind of electricity that can shock you when you touch a doorknob) between a cloud and the ground, other clouds, or within a cloud. Scientists do not yet understand exactly how lightning works, or how it interacts with the upper atmosphere, or the earth's electromagnetic field. Lightning is extremely dangerous, and its hazards should never be lightly regarded. There are some 16 million lightning storms in the world each year. Lightning is one of the oldest and most enigmatic observed natural phenomena on earth. It has been seen in volcanic eruptions, extremely intense forest fires, surface nuclear detonations, heavy snowstorms, in large hurricanes, and obviously, thunderstorms. Humans can be hit by lightning directly when outdoors. Contrary to popular notion, there is no "safe" location outdoors. People have been struck in sheds and makeshift shelters. However, safe shelter is possible within an enclosure of conductive material such as an automobile, which is one example of a crude type of Faraday cage. Lightning can also strike without rain actually falling. If thunder can be heard at all, then there is a risk of lightning. The safest place to be in a lightning storm is inside a building or a vehicle. Risk remains for up to 30 minutes after the last observed lightning or thunder. Lightning strikes can produce severe injuries, and have a mortality rate of between 10% and 30%, with up to 80% of survivors sustaining long-term injuries. An estimated 24,000 people are killed by lightning strikes around the world each year, and about 240,000 are injured. From this discharge of atmospheric electricity, a leader of a bolt of lightning can travel at speeds of 220,000 km/h (140,000 mph), and can reach temperatures approaching 30,000 °C (54,000 °F), hot enough to fuse silica sand into glass. Lightning is the second most deadly weather-related hazard that occurs in the U.S. A person injured by lightning does not carry an electrical charge, and can be safely handled to apply first aid before emergency services arrive. Lightning can affect the brainstem, which controls breathing. If a victim appears lifeless, it is important to begin artificial resuscitation immediately to prevent death by suffocation.

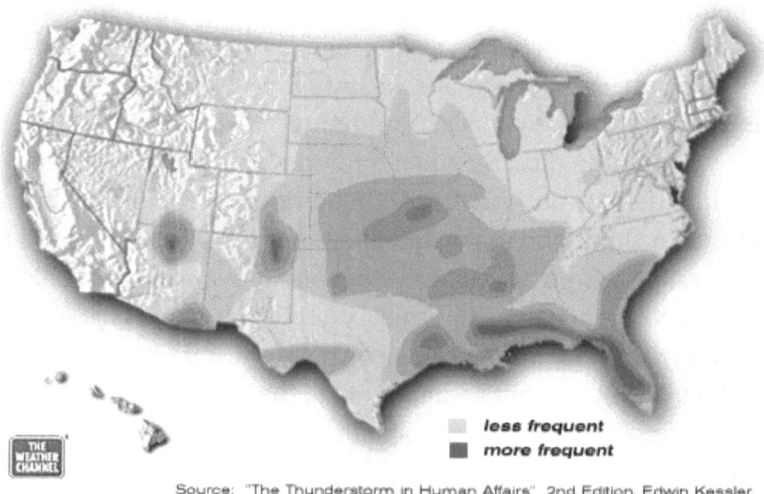

LIGHTNING INCIDENCE MAP
Annual frequency of cloud-to-ground lightning.

less frequent
more frequent

Source: "The Thunderstorm in Human Affairs" 2nd Edition, Edwin Kessler, Editor University of Oklahoma Press, Norman, OK, 1983

Safety tip: Never, ever take shelter from lightning under a tree.

Lightning facts

- 16 million lightning storms occur in the world each year.
- Africa and Brazil have the highest number of lightning strikes.
- 25 million cloud-to-ground lightning strikes occur in the United States each year.
- The air within a lightning strike can reach 50,000 degrees Fahrenheit.
- Lightning can heat its path five times hotter than the surface of the Sun.
- One ground lightning strike can generate between 100 million and 1 billion volts of electricity.
- The mortality rate for a lightning strike is between 10 and 30%.

Lightning and storm risk worldwide

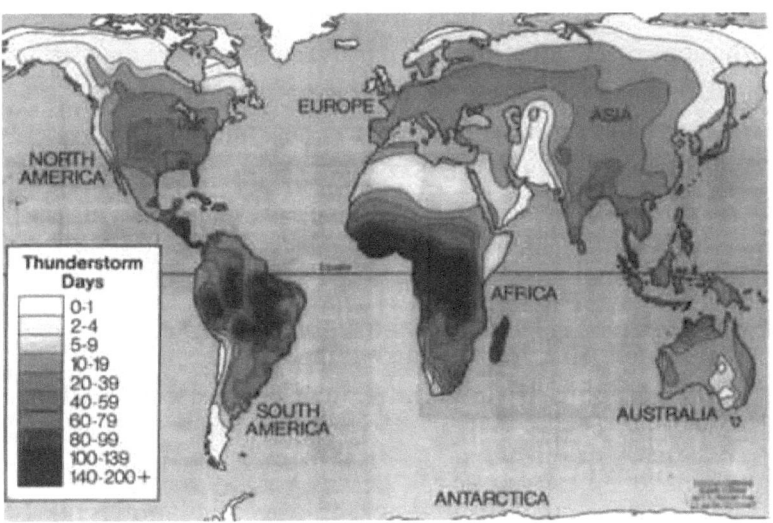

Blizzard – the rage of snowstorms

A blizzard is characterized as a severe snowstorm with strong blowing winds, and low temperatures. Blizzards can occur anywhere it snows, but they are particularly prevalent in regions that receive heavy snowfalls. By definition, the difference between a blizzard and a snowstorm is the strength of the wind blowing the snow. To be a blizzard, a snow storm must have sustained winds or frequent gusts that are greater than, or equal to 56 km/h (35 mph) with blowing or drifting snow, which reduces visibility to 400 meters or a quarter mile or less; and it must last for a prolonged period of time — typically three hours or more. Snowfall amounts generally do not have to be significant. In Australia, a blizzard, by definition, generally contains at least some snow that has been raised from the ground. A severe blizzard has winds over 72 km/h (45 mph), near zero visibility, and temperatures of −12 °C (10 °F) or lower. A ground blizzard has snowdrifts and blowing snow near the ground, but no falling snow. Blizzards can bring near-whiteout conditions, and can paralyze regions for days at a time, particularly where snowfall is unusual or rare. The 1972 Iran blizzard, which caused approximately 4,000 deaths, was the deadliest blizzard in recorded history.

Types of storms

- Snow Flurries – Light snow falling for short durations. No accumulation or light dusting is all that is expected.
- Snow Showers – Snow falling at varying intensities for brief periods of time. Some accumulation is possible.

- Snow Squalls – Brief, intense snow showers accompanied by strong, gusty winds. Accumulation may be significant. Snow squalls are best known in the Great Lakes Region.
- Blowing Snow – Wind-driven snow that reduces visibility and causes significant drifting. Blowing snow may be snow that is falling and/or loose snow on the ground picked up by the wind.
- Blizzard – Winds over 35mph with snow and blowing snow, reducing visibility to 1/4 mile or less for at least 3 hours.

The Defense

HAZARD THREAT

Most people that are killed in blizzards are either taken by complete surprise by the unexpected weather, or they were ill-prepared for its arrival. 70% of the deaths that take place during a blizzard also happen to people who are traveling during a winter storm. If you are traveling anywhere during the winter months, make sure you know the forecast for the duration of your stay. You can tune into daily updates by shortwave radio, local news, or the internet. If you are in a remote wilderness park, routinely check for updates with park officials; and always bring maps and emergency signaling equipment and supplies in case your car breaks down.

Trapped in a vehicle

- Never drive in a snow storm or blizzard if there is near zero visibility. Pull over to the side of the road to avoid an accident or collision with other another vehicle.
- Stay inside your car. Find ways to signal for help with a phone call or emergency beacons. If you have a long

work commute that could potentially put you in peril of being stuck in a snow storm- always make sure your mobile phone is charged fully before leaving work. Try to leave work early under such cases to avoid getting stranded.

- Keep your car filled with gas during the winter months, especially in regions where there are frigid cold temperatures and snow. If you get stranded, routinely turn your heater on — but keep a window cracked to avoid potential carbon monoxide poisoning. Don't leave the heater on for more than 10 minutes every half hour to conserve gas.
- Keep emergency supplies in the trunk of your vehicle which includes non-perishable food, water, blankets, flashlights, emergency hazard signs, a hand-crank radio, and some self-warming chemical packs.
- If you are in heavy snowdrifts, check your tailpipe routinely before you turn your heater on, to be sure that it's not blocked with snow, ice, mud, or flooded water. Once it becomes blocked, it can send carbon monoxide into the vehicle and kill you. Since it is odorless and colorless you would have no way of knowing. Most victims of carbon monoxide poisoning simply fall asleep and die.
- Keep your seatbelt on if you're sitting in a car parked on the side of the road. You could be rear-ended by another vehicle.
- Routinely, get out of the car and move around to keep your blood circulating.
- Try to stay hydrated. If you don't have water with you and need to use the snow, be sure to try to melt it before drinking it, because snow can lower your body

temperature when you're trying to survive by maintaining body warmth.

- Turn the overhead light in your vehicle on so that emergency officials can find you. Consequently, it should be mentioned that the best time to change an aging car battery is before the onset of winter.

Hiking or mountain climbing

Learn about the terrain you plan to spend time in. You are in the mountain's domain, and if you go into the experience unprepared with the attitude of a conqueror, you may not live to tell others about your conquest. The forces of nature are mercurial on mountains, especially at higher elevations where the air thins considerably. Be ready for incremental weather. Even in the summer, the mountains can experience sudden storms, including snow storms, which can abruptly materialize out of nowhere. Never go up to the mountains with only light clothing. Always bring warm clothes to put on, should a storm create poor conditions.

- Bring materials to start a fire and have extra warm or chemical heat packs.
- This might sound simple, but it could be a life-saver in the event of a blizzard. Invest in a diving wet suit for a couple of hundred dollars. Most are composed of rubber or composite materials that insulate the body, and thus prevents heat loss. At the very least, it could prevent hypothermia. Keep it stuffed in your back-pack for an emergency situation.
- Have a compass, map, and GPS navigational device with you so you can find your way in the event snow covers trails that you used extensively in your climb.

- Have a distress locator beacon, and never climb a mountain without one, no matter how many times you've explored it before. Incremental weather can change the equation in a moment's notice, putting you in a life and death struggle with the harsh elements of nature. A Mountain Locator Unit (or MLU) is a radio transmitter designed to be used by mountain climbers, as an emergency locator beacon, when the wearer needs rescue. A PLB (or Personal Locator Beacon) forms the same function. A simple laser pointer can also function as a low-tech distress beacon that can be used to signal someone over a great distance, especially at night.

Put arms across face to create air pocket.

Try to penetrate the surface with arm.

33% of all avalanche victims are killed by the trauma of the fall. Avalanches can move at speeds of between 60 and 80 mph. In the event you are ever the victim of an avalanche, and get buried under the snow, put your arms across your face to create an air pocket and remain calm to conserve oxygen. Your best chances of survival involve getting out of the snow, or being rescued before the snow settles in and packs tight around you.

Things you'll need

In addition to the traditional camping items you'll need, here are a few other accessories that shouldn't be overlooked if you plan on venturing up a mountainside. Make sure you go with someone experienced, and take a survival class before you make your trek.

- Warm clothing
- Blankets
- Flashlights and batteries
- Radio
- Compass & GPS device
- Personal Locator Beacon
- Wet suit
- Fire items
- Non perishable food
- Mountain climbing and/or hiking equipment
- First aid kit
- Water
- Binoculars
- Rope
- Shovel
- Avalanche probe
- Avalanche air bag
- Laser pointer
- Tent
- Camping knife
- Mountain sleeping bag
- Mountain walking sticks
- Maps and/or terrain survey charts
- Tarps

Geophysical Earth: Survival depends largely on knowing the planet's many physical characteristics, and knowing how to use them to help aid in your survival.

Ocean Currents World

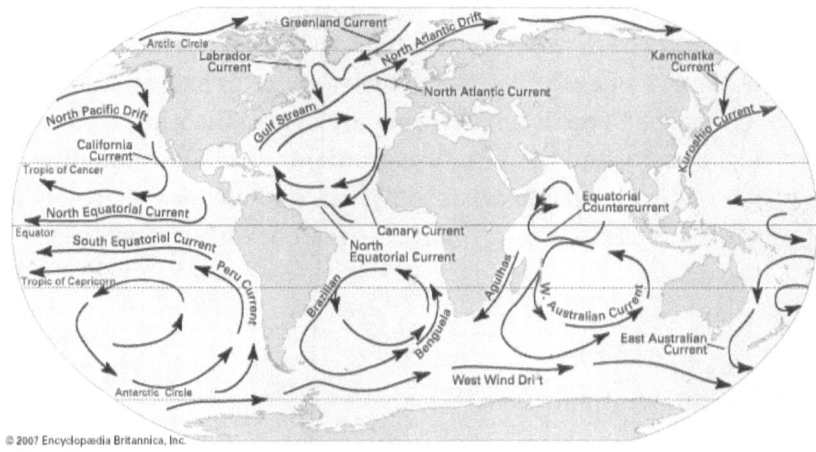

© Map courtesy Encyclopedia Britannica

Ocean currents are continuous multi-directional movements of ocean water, which are generated by the forces acting upon them in terms of; mean flow, breaking waves, the wind, the Coriolis effect, cabbeling, temperature and salinity differences, and tides caused by the gravitational pull of both the Moon and the Sun. Depth contours, shoreline configurations, and interaction with other currents, can greatly influence a current's direction and strength. For the most part, surface ocean currents are generally wind-driven and develop typical clockwise spirals in the northern hemisphere, and counter-clockwise rotation in the southern hemisphere because of the imposed wind stresses. In wind-driven currents, the Ekman spiral effect results in the currents flowing at an angle to the driving winds. The areas of surface ocean currents move somewhat with the seasons;

this is most notable in equatorial currents. Ocean basins generally have a non-symmetric surface current, in that the eastern equatorward-flowing branch is broad and diffuse; whereas the western poleward-flowing branch is very narrow. These western boundary currents (of which the Gulf Stream is an example) are a consequence of basic fluid dynamics. Deep ocean currents are driven by other factors like density and temperature gradients. The Thermohaline circulation, also known as the ocean's conveyor belt, refers to the deep ocean, density-driven, ocean basin currents under the ocean.

Global wind patterns – Earth

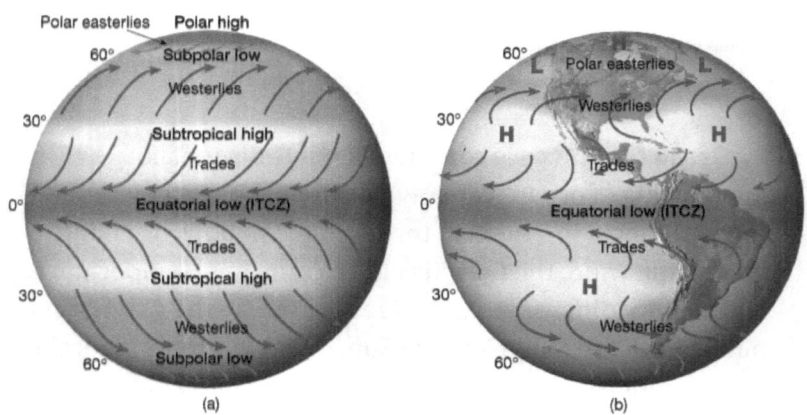

(a)   (b)

Wind Patterns

Understanding wind patterns is extremely important because it's a crucial determinate factor in regard to mitigating some of the risks associated with natural disasters, volcanic eruptions, geological hazards, and environmental contamination; be it chemical or radioactive fallout. Depending on where you're located on the globe, a major volcanic eruption, a hurricane or cyclone, or even hazardous chemical and radiation fallout, all follow wind patterns. You can avoid contact or contamination, and mitigate your risks from some of these hazards by traveling in the opposite direction of wind flows. A Yellowstone or Long Valley supervolcano eruption in the U.S., for instance, would blow ash clouds from west to east. Volcanic ash clouds, on the other hand, from volcanoes erupting in Central America would be caught up in the mid-tropical trade winds and would blow from east to west.

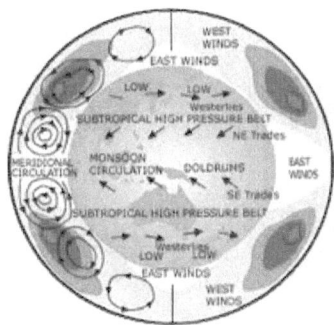

Tectonic Plates

The lithosphere of the planet is broken up into many tectonic plates. On Earth, there are seven or eight major tectonic plates, and many minor plates which are sometimes referred to as micro or sub-plates. Where plates meet, their relative motion determines the type of boundary. Convergent plates undergo subduction, where one plate slides under the other, as is the case with the Nazca and South American

Plate. Divergent plates pull apart, as is the case with the North American and Eurasian plates, or transform and slide past each other, as is the case with the San Andreas Fault of California or the Alpine Fault of New Zealand. Earthquakes, volcanic activity, orogeny, and oceanic trench formation occur along these plate boundaries. The lateral relative movement of the plates typically varies from zero to 100 mm annually.

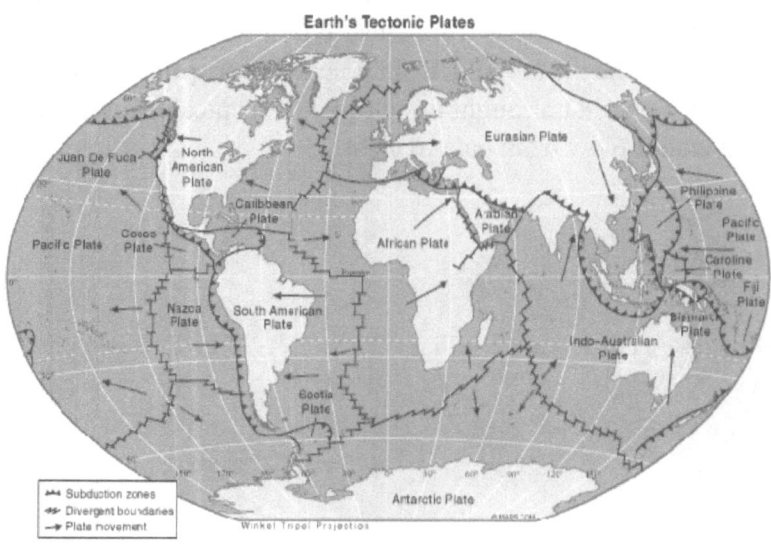

Earth's Tectonic Plates

- North American Plate
- South American Plate
- Pacific Plate
- Nazca Plate
- Indo-Australian Plate
- Antarctica Plate
- African Plate
- Eurasian Plate

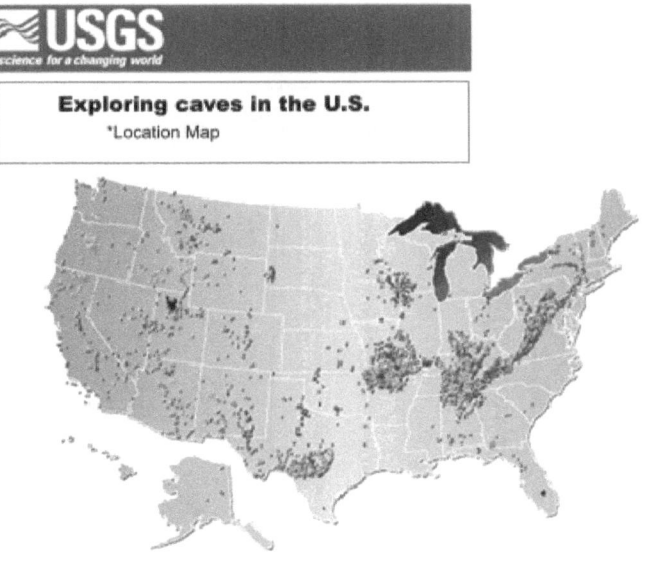

Exploring caves in the U.S.
*Location Map

Caves U.S.

Caves can become emergency shelters in the event of a major natural disaster, such as a nuclear detonation, or a supervolcanic eruption. There are thousands of caves in the United States, including a number that are of spectacular proportions. Mammoth Cave, in Kentucky, has over 300 miles of passageways. Carlsbad Caverns, in New Mexico, has a cavern that is the size of eight football fields. Most American caves are found in limestone rock. The caves began as water made cracks in the limestone, and the cracks got bigger and bigger. The opening grew into underwater streams and rivers. When the water was gone, these underground waterways became cave tunnels and caverns. It can take from 10,000 to 100,000 years to make a cave that is large enough for humans to explore.

Aquifers

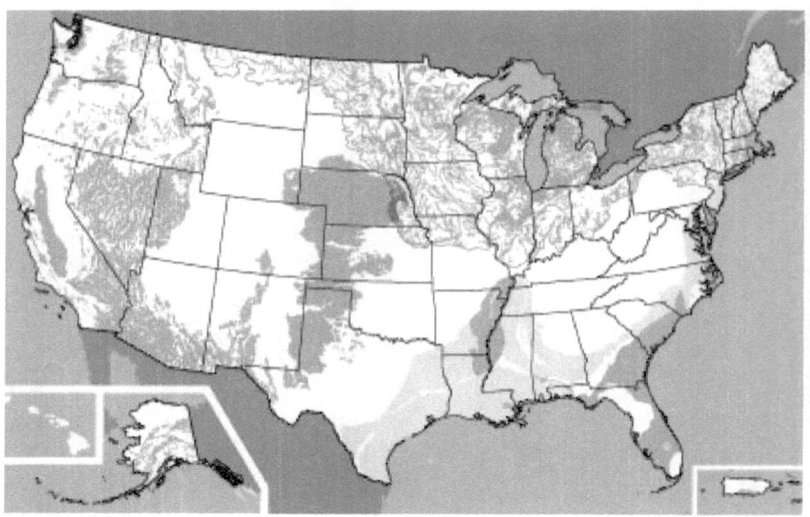

Sand and gravel aquifer map of U.S. where water tables are shallower; and *below*, aquifers in Europe and Africa

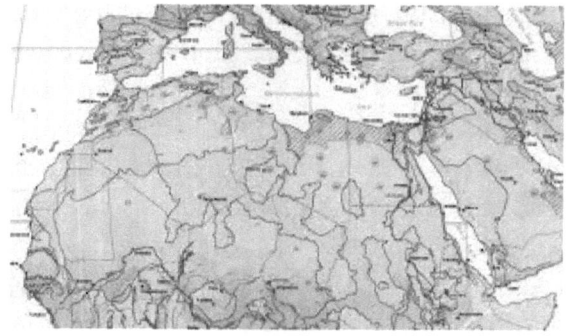

An aquifer is an underground layer of water-bearing permeable rock or unconsolidated materials (gravel, sand, or silt) from which groundwater can be extracted.

Location of the world's geothermal geysers

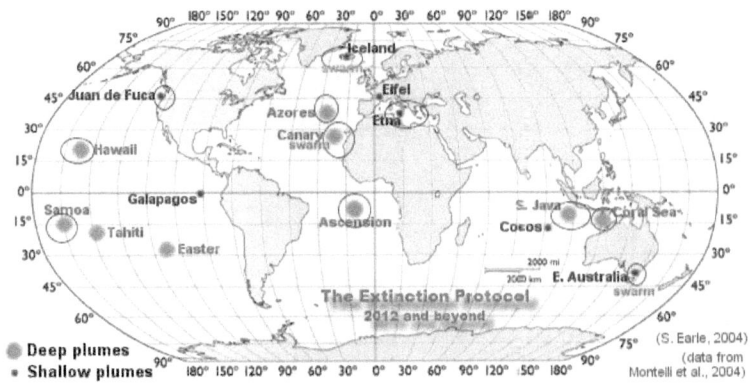

Mantle Plume: A mantle plume is a massive upwelling of abnormally hot rock within the Earth's mantle. These regions are also called *hot-spots* and represents plumes that transfer magma from the outer core to upper mantle. Mantle plumes are important geological features that dissipate planetary heat.

Infrastructure: navigating what connects the world

Stay on these roads – U.S. Interstate Highway System

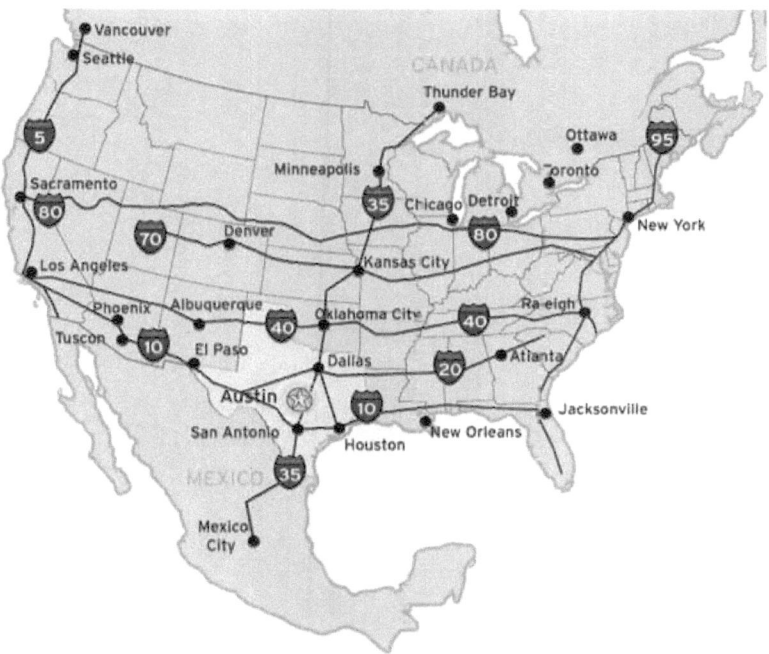

It is still considered one of the largest construction projects in recorded history. The Dwight D. Eisenhower National System of Interstate and Defense Highways (commonly known as the Interstate Highway System, Interstate Freeway System or the Interstate) is a network of limited-access roads, including freeways, highways, and expressways, forming part of the National Highway System of the United States. The system is named for President Dwight D. Eisenhower, who championed its formation. Construction was authorized by the Federal Aid Highway Act of 1956, and the original portion was completed 35 years later. The network has since been extended, and as of 2010, it had a total length of 47,182 miles (75,932 km). In case you're ever lost, always remember, odd numbered interstates run north and south, and even numbered interstates run east and west.

Natural gas network

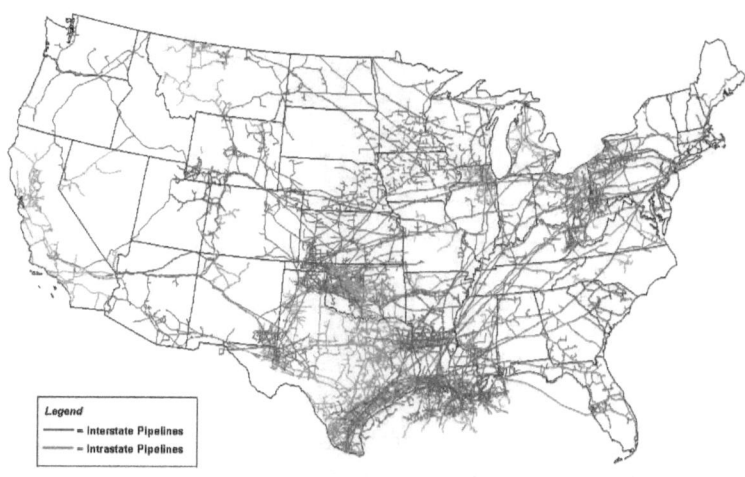

Legend
——— = Interstate Pipelines
——— = Intrastate Pipelines

Source: Energy Information Administration, Office of Oil & Gas, Natural Gas Division, Gas Transportation Information System

Natural Gas pipeline network: In the likelihood of large-scale seismic events, you will want to know where natural gas pipelines are that crisscross the U.S., so you can avoid any potential hazards, if massive explosive fires occur or erupt. Many of the pipelines run along, or near, fault zones including New Madrid and San Andreas, as well as along the corridor of East Texas.

COUNTRIES AFFECTED BY CRISIS

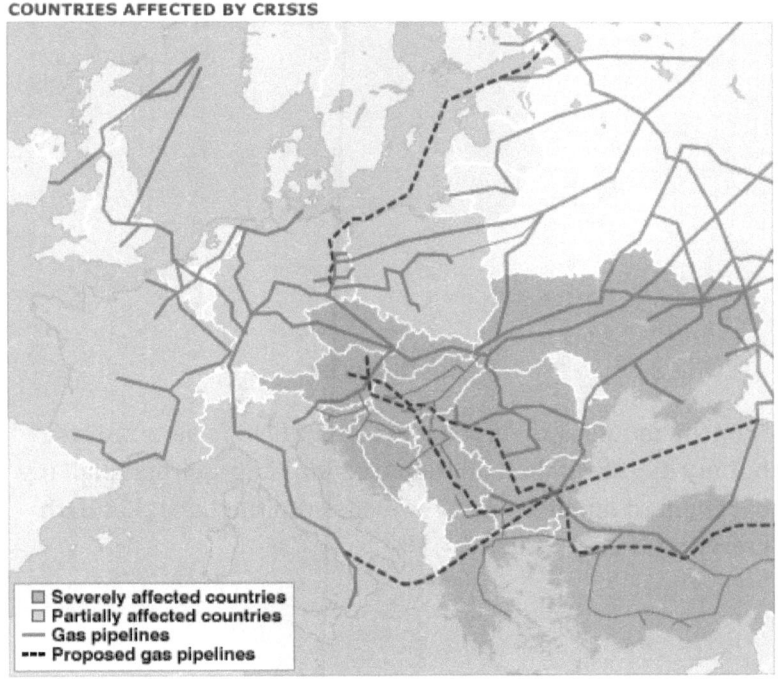

Natural Gas pipelines Europe – credit BBC

PLANNED SOUTH STREAM AND NABUCCO GAS PIPELINES

Earthquakes and Seismic Hazards

Earthquake

"For the mountains shall depart, and the hills be removed; but my kindness shall not depart from thee, neither shall my covenant of my peace be removed, saith the Lord that hath mercy on thee." –Isaiah 54:10

Earthquakes – When the Earth Shakes

An earthquake is surface-tension motion caused by a sudden release of energy in the Earth's crust that creates seismic waves. At the Earth's surface, earthquakes can cause the ground to shake or sometimes rise, in what's known as an uplift. It can also fall in a subsidence or split in two in a rift. If the epicenter of a large earthquake is located offshore, the seabed may be displaced sufficiently to cause a tsunami. Earthquakes can also trigger landslides, and frequently they can ignite volcanic activity. Approximately 90% of all earthquake epicenters are at a depth of less than 100 km; whereas only about 3% of all earthquakes are deep. Sometimes the shaking from an earthquake can be horizontal and sometimes it can be vertical. In rare cases, both can occur and in these instances, *liquefaction* may result. Liquefaction occurred in both the February 2011 6.3 Christchurch New Zealand earthquake, and the 9.0 March 11, 2011 Honshu earthquake, which struck Japan. Soil liquefaction occurs when, because of the shaking, water-saturated granular material (such as sand) temporarily loses its strength and transforms from a solid to a liquid. Soil liquefaction may cause rigid structures, like buildings and bridges, to tilt or sink into the liquefied deposits. This can intensify the devastating effect of earthquakes. For example, in the 1964 9.2 Alaska earthquake, soil liquefaction caused many buildings to sink into the ground, eventually collapsing upon themselves.

The Alaskan earthquake lasted nearly four minutes, and it was the most powerful earthquake ever recorded in the U.S. and North America. The violent toll the quake exacted on the landscape, almost defies imagination. Near Kodiak, Alaska, parts of the ground were permanently raised by 30 feet (9.1 m). Southeast of Anchorage, areas around the head of Turnagain Arm near Girdwood and Portage dropped as much as 8 feet (2.4 m).

About **90%** of the world's earthquakes and **80%** of the world's largest earthquakes occur along the Ring of Fire. The next most active seismic region (5–6% of earthquakes and 17% of the world's largest earthquakes) is the *Alpide belt*, which extends from Java to Sumatra through the Himalayas, the Mediterranean, and out into the Atlantic. The Mid-Atlantic Ridge is the third most prominent earthquake belt.

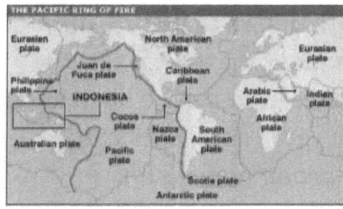 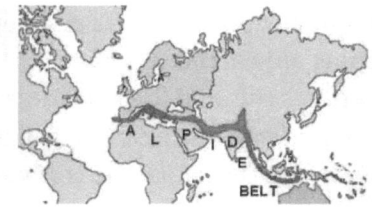

Seismic Danger Zones: (Left) the Pacific Ring of Fire and the Alpide Belt (Right)

The Defense

Hazard Threat

Risk Mitigation: Earthquakes can strike suddenly and with very little warning. If you live in a high-risk earthquake region of the world, you should always be prepared for the eventuality of an earthquake. Have a disaster plan in place before the earthquake strikes. As geologic change intensifies across our planet, the perils from large earthquake strikes will increase, particularly in large urban areas situated in seismic zones. The list of helpful tips, on the next page, is designed to mitigate potential risks associated with an earthquake.

Before an earthquake:

- It is important to learn about safety and hazards before an earthquake strikes. Most small earthquakes last only seconds but generally the larger the earthquake, the longer the shaking will last because of the proportionate amount of energy that is displaced through the ground from a fault eruption.

- Have an earthquake plan and routinely practice it in drills. Remember these points: **1**) Know what you are going to do when the shaking occurs, **2**) Designate safe places, such as under a strong desk, along interior walls, and open ground, and **3**) Avoid places prone to hazards, like near windows, basements, in the vicinity of large mirrors, hanging objects, balconies or top floors of buildings.

- Have emergency supplies. These include: battery-operated or hand-cranked radio (and extra batteries), flashlights (hand-cranked and extra batteries), a first aid kit, bottled water, 3 to 14 day supply of food and medicals, blankets, cooking fuel, essential tools needed to turn off your gas, water, or power in the event of a leak, damage, or breach.

- If you live in a high-risk earthquake area, arrange your home to survive an evacuation if it is ever struck by an earthquake. Avoid hanging heavy pictures or chandeliers over stairwells. Also keep staircases free from heavy objects that could overturn and impede your evacuation, like grandfather clocks and bookcases.

- It is wise to have heavy appliances and furniture such as water heaters, refrigerators and bookcases anchored or bolted securely, so they won't overturn in the event of an earthquake.

- Earthquake-proof your home: Windows are usually the first causalities of a major earthquake, and broken glass could become a hazard in an evacuation zone. In the event of an earthquake, windows will break from general impact or any of the three movement factors of: vibration, expansion, and buckling. You can get earthquake safety glass or have blinds installed which would impede the effects of flying shards of glass.

- Always store flammable liquids away from potential ignition sources such as water heaters, stoves and furnaces.

- Know your utility check points. Learn where the main turn-off valves and/ or switches are for your water, gas and electricity. Know how to turn them off, and the location of any needed tools to service them in the event of an emergency.

- If you work in a high rise, familiarize yourself with all the emergency evacuation plans.

During an earthquake:

- If you are indoors, stay there. Seek shelter in a safe location of the room such as under a strong desk, a strong table, or along an interior wall. Protect yourself from falling objects and tree limbs crashing through windows. Do your best to be located near the structural strong points of the house. Do not take cover near windows, gas appliances, large mirrors, hanging objects, heavy furniture, heavy appliances, stone fireplaces or in a basement or elevators.

- Stay clear of utility connections near buildings, and avoid power lines running near trees.

- If you are driving, slow down smoothly and stop on the side of the road, as the motion of the road will overwhelm the steering of your car. Do not park near railroad tracks or under bridges, trestles, overpasses, power lines, trees or large signs. Stay in your car to avoid electrocution, especially if live power lines or transformers have fallen near you.

After the earthquake:

- Call emergency medical personnel in the event of an accident, severe damage, or bodily injury. Prepare to render CPR or first aid on your family members or people around you if the need should arise. Cardiac arrests are common occurrences in earthquakes.

- Do an initial damage assessment of your property. If you smell gas, open the windows and evacuate the house. Place a call to emergency officials if there is a leak. If you see downed power lines, evacuate your premises immediately and call emergency or utility personnel to make a report. You should keep a list of utility companies' emergency numbers in your phone and also in your emergency kit, in case phone service has been disrupted. The list should also include the policy number and the phone number of your insurance agent. If your building is badly damaged, you should also evacuate it until it has been inspected by a safety professional to make sure it's structurally sound before you re-enter.

- If the power has been disrupted, unplug major appliances to prevent possible damage when the power is turned back on. If you see sparks, frayed wires, or smell hot insulation; turn off the electricity at the main fuse box or breaker if you can reach it safely. Never step in water to turn off the electricity. If the environment has been rendered unsafe, you should call a professional to turn it off for you.

New Madrid Earthquake Fault Zone

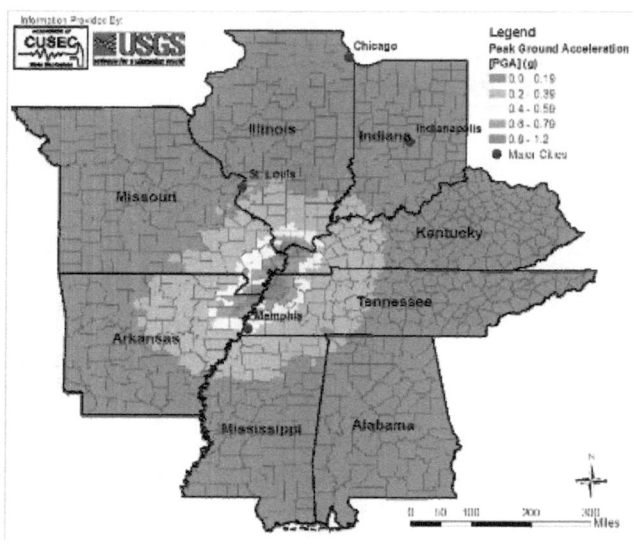

New Madrid Fault – U.S.

The New Madrid seismic zone experienced four of the largest quakes to strike North America in recorded history. The famed 8.0 Madrid earthquakes of 1811-1812 were said to be so powerful, they disrupted the flow of the Mississippi River. Of particular cause for concern are the eyewitness accounts of the duration of the shaking from the 1811 quake that struck this fault- reports said the shaking lasted 10-12 minutes. Compared with the 90 seconds of the 2010 Chile and Haiti earthquakes- that's an apocalyptic length of time, considering this region of the U.S. is so densely populated today.

There are some 200 quakes reported along the New Madrid fault every year. The last notable earthquake occurred when a 5.2 magnitude quake struck near Bellmont, Illinois in 2008. Though the epicenter of the quake was 160 miles north of New Madrid's center; tremors were reported in 26 states, and as far away as Florida. That's an indication of just how dangerous and fractured these fault lines are. According to geologists, a major quake along the New Madrid fault is long overdue. A dark, sinister cloud still lingers over the region. A report filed in November of 2008 by the U.S Federal Emergency Management Agency warned that a major earthquake in the New Madrid Fault region would be one of the costliest disasters in U.S. history. A June 2010 study by the University of Illinois reached a similar conclusion. According to the University of Illinois study, a 7.7 magnitude earthquake along the New Madrid fault would:

- Kill 3,500 people and leave 80,000 injured

- Leave 7 million people homeless

- Destroy 715,000 buildings, and render 15 nuclear plants inoperable

- Leave 2.6 million people without electricity

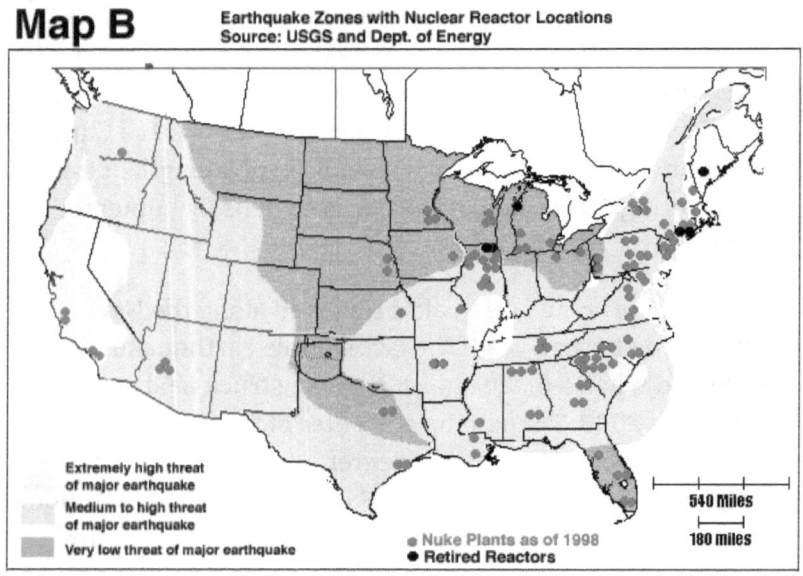

Map B Earthquake Zones with Nuclear Reactor Locations
Source: USGS and Dept. of Energy

The dangers of nuclear plants being located in high-risk disaster zones were made painfully obvious with the Fukushima nuclear plant disaster in Japan. Nuclear plants consume huge amounts of water that is used in the cooling system to keep the reactor from over-heating. A meltdown occurs when there is a severe nuclear reactor accident which results in core damage from overheating. A core melt accident occurs when the heat generated by a nuclear reactor exceeds the heat removed by the cooling systems to the point where at least one nuclear fuel element exceeds its melting point. Most nuclear reactors operate with primary back-up generators, and if these fail, a secondary system of diesel generators is used. However, in the massive 9.0 earthquake and tsunami which struck off the east coast of Japan, both of these primary and secondary cooling systems failed. What followed was the core could not be cooled fast enough. Japanese workers in desperation, began dumping hundreds of thousands of liters of seawater into the reactor in a vain attempt to cool them. However, this failed and the reactors went into meltdown mode. The nuclear accident at the Fukushima Daiichi plant, the worst since Chernobyl, triggered fuel meltdowns at three of its six reactors, and caused a huge radiation leak that has displaced as many as 100,000 people. It will take about 30 years to contain the accident at the Fukushima plant, if it ever can be contained at all. Even worse, hazardous radiation from the disaster has already seeped into the environment, and its detrimental effects will linger for a hundred years or more.

Fukushima has become a cautionary tale of what can happen to even the so-called best, well constructed nuclear power plants built in high-risk seismic zones. Nothing manufactured by man can contend with the powerful forces of nature unleashed in a large-scale cataclysmic event. A major earthquake in the New Madrid fault zone could create a similar Fukushima-style scenario for the U.S. There are 15 nuclear reactors located within the hazardous region of the New Madrid Fault zone.

Nuclear plants worldwide – 2012 study risks are rising

"Catastrophic nuclear accidents such as the core meltdowns in Chernobyl and Fukushima are more likely to happen than previously assumed. Based on the operating

hours of all civil nuclear reactors and the number of nuclear
meltdowns that have occurred, scientists at the Max Planck
Institute for Chemistry in Mainz have calculated that such
events may occur once every 10 to 20 years (based on the
current number of reactors) — some 200 times more often
than estimated in the past. The researchers also determined
that, in the event of such a major plant accident, half of the
radioactive caesium-137 would be spread over an area of
more than 1,000 kilometers away from the nuclear reactor.

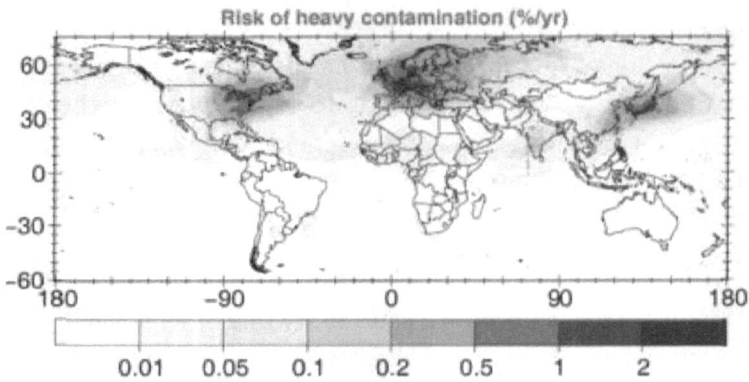

Probability of contamination from nuclear reactor accident – Credit:
Daniel Kunkel, MPI for Chemistry, 2011

Their results show that Western Europe is likely to be
contaminated about once in 50 years by more than 40
kilobecquerel of caesium-137 per square meter. According to
the International Atomic Energy Agency, an area is defined as
being contaminated with radiation from this amount
onwards. In view of their findings, the researchers call for an
in-depth analysis and reassessment of the risks associated
with nuclear power plants. According to the results of the
study, a nuclear meltdown in one of the reactors in operation
worldwide is likely to occur once in 10 to 20 years. Currently,

there are 440 nuclear reactors in operation, and 60 more are planned." [1]

The world's most dangerous seismic faults

- **Cascadia Subduction Zone** – Cascadia runs along the NW coast of U.S. and Canada. The Cascadia subduction zone (also referred to as the Cascadia fault), is a type of convergent plate boundary that stretches from northern Vancouver Island to northern California. It is a very long sloping fault that separates the Juan de Fuca and North America plates. The fault is capable of generating earthquakes in the 8.0 to 9.0 + magnitude range.
- **San Andreas Fault** – California. The San Andreas Fault is a continental transform fault that runs a length of roughly 810 miles (1,300 km) through California in the United States. It is one of the most dangerous faults in North America. The fault's motion is right-lateral strike-slip (horizontal motion). It forms the tectonic boundary between the Pacific Plate and the North American Plate The San Andreas is capable of generating earthquakes in the 8.0 + magnitude range.
- **Alpine Fault** – New Zealand. The Alpine Fault is a geological fault, more specifically known as a right-lateral strike-slip fault, which runs almost the entire length of New Zealand's South Island. It forms a transform boundary between the Pacific Plate and the Indo-Australian Plate. The fault is capable of generating earthquakes in the magnitude of 7.9.
- **Denali Fault – Alaska**. The Denali Fault is a major intra-continental dextral (right lateral) strike-slip

fault in western North America, extending from northwestern British Columbia, Canada to the U.S. state of central Alaska. The fault is capable of generating earthquakes from the 7.0 to the upper 8.0 magnitude range.

- **North Anatolia Fault** – Turkey. The North Anatolian Fault (NAF) (Turkish: *Kuzey Anadolu Fay Hattı*) is a major active right-lateral moving strike-slip fault in northern Anatolia which runs along the transform boundary between the Eurasian Plate and the Anatolian Plate. The fault extends westward from a junction with the East Anatolian Fault at the Karliova Triple Junction in eastern Turkey, across northern Turkey and into the Aegean Sea. It runs about 20 km south of Istanbul. This is a very dangerous fault that is capable of producing 7.0 to 8.0 magnitude quakes.
- **Laguna Salada Fault** – Southern California. The Laguna Salada Fault is a geological fault that runs between the United States and Mexico. About 64 kilometers (40 mi) to 80 kilometers (50 mi) long, it straddles the Imperial County, California–Baja, California border. The fault was responsible for the 7.2 magnitude Baja, California earthquake of 2010.
- **Hayward Fault Zone** –Northern California. This fault is about 74 mi (119 km) long, situated mainly along the western base of the hills on the east side of San Francisco Bay. It runs through densely populated areas, including the northern cities of Richmond, El Cerrito, Berkeley, Oakland, San Leandro, Hayward, Fremont, and San Jose.
- **Wasatch Fault** – Salt Lake City. The Wasatch Fault is a 240 mile like seismic hazard zone that lies underneath Salt Lake City, Utah, home to some 1.6

million people. Though the Wasatch Fault has not delivered a major earthquake since the Mormon settlers arrived in 1847, geologists have found evidence that the fault is capable of unleashing seismic quakes as big as magnitude 7.5. It is one of the world's longest "normal" faults, where the land on one side of the fault drops down relative to the other side during an earthquake. During prehistoric times, the Wasatch fault is believed to have slipped as much as 10 feet during a single quake.

- **New Madrid** – U.S. Midwest: The New Madrid Seismic Zone, sometimes called the New Madrid Fault Line, is a major seismic zone and a prolific source of intraplate earthquakes (earthquakes within a tectonic plate) in the southern and Midwestern United States, stretching to the southwest from New Madrid, Missouri. The fault erupted from 1811-1812 producing earthquakes in the 7.0 to 8.0 magnitude range. *Below is a map of U.S. seismic risks:*

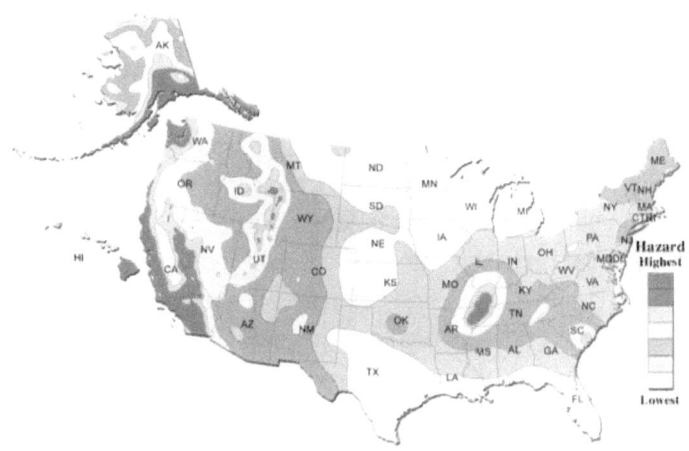

Tectonic plate – Mediterranean region seismicity

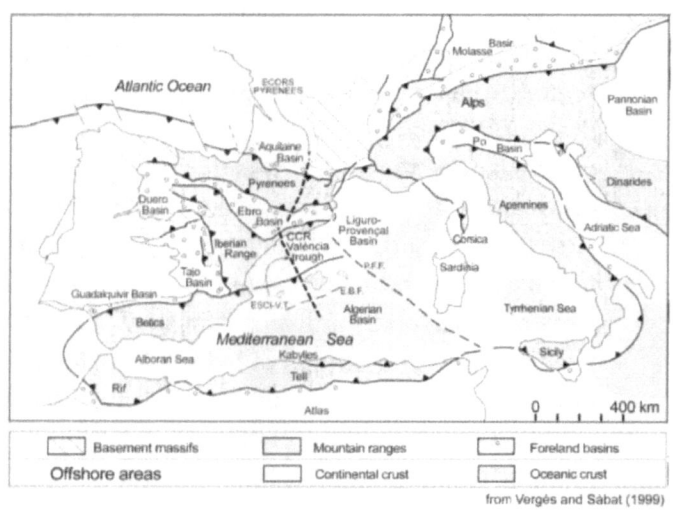

from Vergés and Sábat (1999)

This region of the Mediterranean is destined to see more seismic turbulence according to a report published in April of 2011 by Dutch geophysicist Rinus Wortel. *National Geographic* said: "Europe may be starting to dive under Africa, creating a new subduction zone and potentially increasing the earthquake risk in the western Mediterranean Sea, scientists report. Subduction zones form where tectonic plates collide, with one plate diving beneath the other and into Earth's mantle. Sometimes these collisions are gradual, but often they occur in big lurches that can trigger quakes. Because subduction zones are generally on sea beds, earthquakes in these zones can set off tsunamis, like the killer wave that devastated Japan in 2011. For millions of years the African plate, which contains part of the Mediterranean seabed, has been moving northward toward the Eurasian Plate at a rate of about an inch every 2.5 years (a centimeter a year). Now studies of recent earthquakes in the region indicate that a new subduction zone may be forming where the plates are colliding along the coasts of Algeria and northern Sicily. 'Formation of a new subduction zone is very rare,' said study leader Rinus Wortel, a geophysicist at Utrecht University in the Netherlands... based on the locations and motions of recent earthquakes along the plate borders, Wortel and colleagues think subduction is starting up again, but this time with Europe being thrust under Africa...'For example,' he said, 'most established subduction zones are marked by giant undersea trenches. A *very* similar trench *system* should eventually form in the Mediterranean—but certainly not overnight.' Wortel does believe that the new data may mean the earthquake risk in the western Mediterranean has been underestimated—and may be increasing." [2]

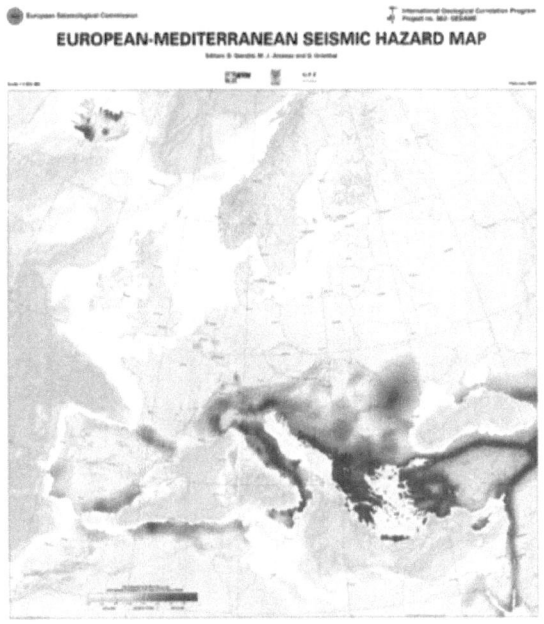

Volcanoes – the rage of mountains of fire

Volcano

"God is our refuge and strength, a very present help in trouble. Therefore will not we fear, though the earth be removed, and though the mountains be carried into the midst of the sea; though the waters thereof roar and be troubled, though the mountains shake with the swelling thereof." –Psalm 46:1- 3

Mountains of Fire – Volcanism

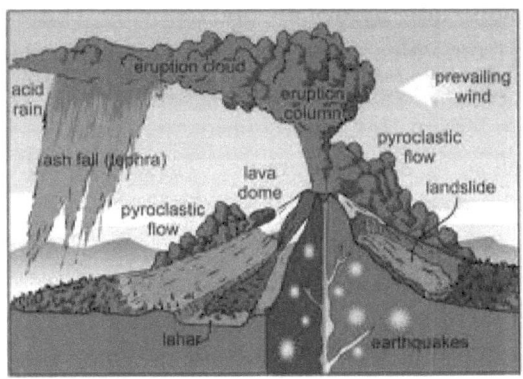

Volcanism is the depressurization of magma in the Earth's crust through vents. Volcanism is one of the basic ways a planet vents or dissipates heat. Fiery volcanic eruptions are quite common on terrestrial rocky planets like Earth. Geologists estimate that there are about 550 volcanoes on land that are considered active. However, the largest number of volcanoes lie under the world's oceans. Oceans covered about 71% of the planet's surface and it is believed that as many as 3 to 4 million volcanoes are lying on the bottom of the sea-floor. Erupting submarine volcanoes can also contribute to the sublimation of frozen methyl hydrate on the ocean floor. Hydrates release huge amounts of methane gas. Methane, or CH_4, is a greenhouse gas that traps about 25 times more of the Sun's heat than CO_2 does. If a large number of volcanoes suddenly erupted under the sea, this could lead to an anoxic event where the oceans are inundated with volcanic gases, and oxygen is depleted from the marine environment. Oceanic anoxic events are said to have occurred during the Cretaceous and Jurassic Periods, when numerous examples have been documented; but earlier examples have been suggested to have occurred during planetary extinction events in the late Triassic, Permian, Devonian, Ordovician, and Cambrian Periods.

Volcanic gases are about 50% to 80% water vapor, with lesser amounts of carbon dioxide, nitrogen, sulfur gases, (especially sulfur dioxide), hydrogen sulfide, and very trace amounts of carbon monoxide, hydrogen, and chlorine. The other danger arising from volcanic eruptions is volcanic ash-pyroclastic particles that measure less than 2.0 mm. In 1947, ash that erupted from Mount Helka in Iceland traveled a great distance and fell some 3,800 kilometers (2,361 miles) away in Helsinki, Finland. Very small ash particles can be less than 0.001 millimeters (1/25,000th of an inch) across. Volcanic ash is not the by-product of combustion, like the soft fluffy material created by burning wood, leaves, or paper. Volcanic ash is hard. It does not dissolve in water. It is extremely abrasive and mildly corrosive, and conducts electricity when wet. The force of the escaping gas from a volcanic eruption violently shatters solid rocks. Expanding gas also shreds magma and blasts it into the air, where it solidifies into fragments of volcanic rock and glass. Volcanic ash is very dangerous because if it is inhaled, the small shards of glass can lacerate the lungs.

1. 60% of all active volcanoes are in the Ring of Fire
2. 20% of all active volcanoes are in the region known as the Mediterranean Belt
3. 20% of all active volcanoes are scattered elsewhere across the globe

Volcanism is responsible for all extrusive igneous rock, such as basalt, tuff, and obsidian. Pompeii, a city of 20,000 people, was only 9 km downwind from Mount Vesuvius and was buried in nearly 3 meters of ash in 79 A.D. Oceanic islands like Hawaii, Iceland, the Canary Islands, and the Azores owe their existence to volcanism. The Pacific Ring of Fire (or just the Ring of Fire) is an area where large numbers of earthquakes and volcanic eruptions occur in the basin of the Pacific Ocean. In a 40,000 km (25,000 mi) horseshoe shape, it is associated with a nearly continuous series of oceanic trenches, volcanic arcs, dense volcanic belts, and/or plate movements. The *Ring of Fire* has **452** volcanoes and is home to over **75%** of the world's active and dormant volcanoes. It is sometimes called the circum-Pacific belt or the circum-Pacific seismic belt. The most dangerous eruptions come from supervolcanoes. A supervolcano is a volcano capable of producing a volcanic eruption with an ejecta volume greater than 1,000 cubic kilometers (240 cubic miles).

The Volcanic Explosivity Index

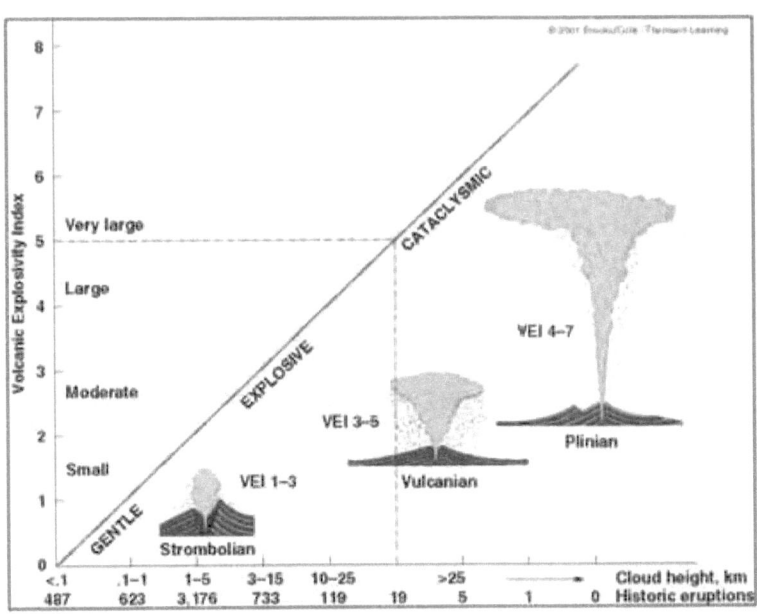

The *Volcanic Explosivity Index*, or VEI, is a scale used to rate the size and scope of a volcanic eruption. The VEI ranges from 0 (gentle) to 8 (cataclysmic) and is based on several criteria of an eruption: the volume of material explosively ejected in an eruption, and the height of the eruption plume. The scale is logarithmic from VEI 2 and up; an increase of 1 index indicates an eruption that is 10 times as powerful. Thus a VEI 3 volcanic eruption is 10 times as powerful as a VEI 2 event and so on. It has been estimated that during the last 10,000 years, 5,700 volcanic eruptions have occurred and about 62% of these were assigned the status of VEI 2. The durations of eruptions vary considerably based on the volcano and the location. Volcanoes in the South America, for instance, tend to erupt longer and eject a thicker type of ash. About 42% of 3,300 historic eruptions lasted less than a month. 33% have erupted from one to six months, and some 16 volcanoes have been active or continuously erupting for more than 20 years. Some volcanoes give little or no warning. Of the 252 or so large historic eruptions ever recorded, a full 42% violently exploded on the first day of activity. The inordinately high number of large, violent volcanic eruptions that happens with relatively little warning underscores the dangers of many large volcanoes.

Types of Magmatic Eruptions ranked by intensity

1. Plinian eruption: very strong eruption – ex: Mt. Pinatubo, the Philippines
2. Peléan eruption: gas, fast-moving pyroclastic flow – ex: Mt. Pelée, Martinique
3. Vulcanian eruption: highly viscous magma flows – ex: Mt. Sakurajima, Japan

4. Strombolian eruptions: lava bombs thrown in the air – ex: Mt. Etna, Sicily (Italy)
5. Hawaiian eruption: effusive eruption where lava oozes – ex: Mt. Kilauea, Hawaii

Large areas can collapse into the ocean with little warning

Dangers from volcanic eruptions

- **Pyroclastic flow** - Pyroclastic flows are avalanches of dense, destructive masses of very hot ash, lava fragments, and gases ejected explosively from a volcano, and typically flowing at speeds which can reach up to 700 km/h (450 mph) with incinerating temperatures of 1,000 °C (1,830 °F). The towns of Pompeii and Herculaneum, Italy, for example, were famously engulfed by pyroclastic surges from the eruption of Mount Vesuvius in 79 AD. Thousands were incinerated instantly by the flows. Pompei, a city of approximately 20,000 people, was only 9 km (5.6 miles) from Mount Vesuvius but the entire city was buried under some 3 meters of pyroclastic material, covering all but the tallest buildings. Herculaneum suffered an even more sinister fate and was buried under ash depths of nearly 20 meters.

- **Poison gas** – In 2000, two people were killed by poison gas, who had taken up casual observer status near a lava stream from Hawaii's Mount Kilauea volcano. Their lungs were swollen and the skin was eaten from their bones by a cloud of hydrochloric acid. Effusive volcanic eruptions create very dangerous conditions because, by all appearances, the oozing lava appears relatively harmless. However, when the lava makes contact with salty sea water, it can turn the chlorine and hydrogen in the water into hydrochloric acid. The toxic cloud of acid is known as lava haze or laze.

- **Tephra** - When lava flows make contact with the sea, the lava is cooled very quickly. The cooling contracts the lava, and the sudden stresses can cause chunks of the lava to fly into the air. These chunks, called tephra, can be lethal aerial debris to anybody standing near a lava water flash point.

- **Boiling seawater** - The temperature of the lava from a volcanic eruption is over 2,000 degrees F. The cooled lava forms shards and lumps, piled unevenly along the shore. New lava flow compacts over this, forming a seemingly solid top layer that, in reality, is very pliable and unstable. It's called a lava bench, and if you're standing on one when it collapses, you could literally be boiled alive in the open sea.

- **Vog** - Vog is dense volcanic gas, ash and mist. Breathing in this haze can create all types of respiratory problems. Vog is a type of air pollution that results when sulfur dioxide and other gases and particles emitted by an erupting volcano react with oxygen and moisture in the presence of sunlight. Mount Kīlauea in Hawaii produces a lot of vog. As a matter of fact, based on 2008 measurements, Kīlauea emits between 2,000 and 4,000 tons of sulfur dioxide gas every day.

- **Lava Tube collapse** - Effusive volcanic eruptions send lava to the oceans via flow streams called lava tubes. The surface of the lava cools while the hot lava flows underneath. Since this is rapidly cooled rock, it can be very brittle, and could easily collapse if you walked on it, applying too much pressure.

- **Suffocation by limnic eruption** – Sometimes volcanoes erupt, not by expelling ash or lava, but by belching large amounts of CO_2. This is known as a limnic overturn. The eruptions are mostly silent and you don't know it has happened, until you drop dead from suffocation. CO_2 gas is colorless and odorless. It's heavier and cooler than air, so it hugs the ground moving in a rapid stream as it fans out from the volcanic crater. In 1986, Lake Nyos in Cameroon had a limnic eruption that killed 1,700 people. The dense cloud of CO_2 gas swept down from the mountain summit and rumbled through a village, killing both man and beast in their tracks.

- **Tephra jets** - Lava that's superheated can eject tephra jets high into the air. The debris can contain lava bombs, as well as shards of glass.

The Mid-Atlantic Ridge (MAR) is a mid-ocean ridge, a divergent tectonic plate boundary about 40,000 km long, located along the floor of the Atlantic Ocean, and is part of the longest mountain range in the world. It separates the Eurasian Plate and North American Plate in the North Atlantic, and the African Plate from the South American Plate in the South Atlantic. The average spreading rate for the ridge is about 2.5 cm (less than 1 inch) per year.

Population density in the Ring of Fire

- Indonesia- 238 million (136 active volcanoes with about 76 erupted in Holocene period)
- Japan- 127 million (Japan has 108 active volcanoes, about 10% of the world's total)
- Philippines- 94 million (37 volcanoes and 18 are considered active)
- Fiji Republic- 900,000 (4 volcanoes – with 2 considered active)
- Vanuatu- 225,000 (4 active volcanoes)

Mount Tambora (or Tamboro) is an active stratovolcano, also known as a composite volcano, on the island of Sumbawa, Indonesia. Sumbawa is flanked both to the north and south by oceanic crust, and Tambora was formed by the active subduction zone beneath it. This raised Mount Tambora as high as 4,300 m (14,100 ft), formerly making it one of the tallest peaks in the Indonesian archipelago. After a large magma chamber inside the mountain filled over the course of several decades, volcanic activity reached a historic climax in the super colossal eruption of April 1815.

The 1815 eruption is rated **7** on the Volcanic Explosivity Index (VEI), the only such eruption since the Lake Taupo eruption in about 180 AD. With an estimated ejecta volume of 160 cubic kilometers, Tambora's 1815 outburst was the largest volcanic eruption in recorded history.

The Hatepe eruption (named for the Hatepe Plinian pumice tephra layer; sometimes referred to as the Taupo eruption) around the year 180 AD was Lake Taupo's most recent major eruption, and New Zealand's largest eruption during the last 20,000 years. It ejected some 120 km³ (29 cu mi) of material (rating a **7** on the Volcanic Explosivity Index scale), of which 30 km³ was ejected in the space of a few minutes.

VEI 8 Events

- **Yellowstone Caldera**, Lava Creek Tuff, Wyoming, United States, Yellowstone hotspot—640,000 years ago.
- **Lake Taupo**, Taupo Volcanic Zone, North Island, New Zealand—Oruanui eruption - 26,500 years ago
- **Lake Toba**, Sumatra, Indonesia - 74,000 years ago
- **La Garita Caldera**, Colorado, United States—Source of the enormous eruption of the Fish Canyon Tuff - 27.8 million years ago

VEI 6 Events

- Krakatoa (1883), and Mount Pinatubo (1991), after lying dormant for 600 years

The Supervolcanoes

There are currently seven known supervolcanoes on the planet: The Yellowstone, Long Valley, and Valles calderas in the United States; Lake Toba, North Sumatra, Indonesia;

Taupo Volcano, North Island, New Zealand; and Aira Caldera, Kagoshima Prefecture, Kyūshū, Japan. Although there are only a handful of Quaternary supervolcanoes, supervolcanic eruptions typically cover huge areas with lava and volcanic ash, and cause a long-lasting change to weather (such as the triggering of a small ice age) sufficient to threaten the extinction of species. A supervolcano is a volcano capable of producing a volcanic eruption with ejecta greater than 1,000 cubic kilometers (240 cubic miles). I suspect there are many more such volcanoes lying under the world's oceans that have not been undiscovered. As a matter of fact, the world's oceans may be more predisposed to the formation of supervolcanoes because the crust under the world's oceans is much thinner. Submarine supervolcanoes may have also played a huge and completely overlooked role in the great Anoxic Event which robbed oceans completely of oxygen eons ago.

- Yellowstone- Wyoming
- Long Valley- California
- Leguna del Maule – Chile
- Lake Toba – North Sumatra, Indonesia
- Lake Taupo- North Island, New Zealand
- Uturuncu – Bolivia
- Campi Flegrei – Italy

Total Number of Volcanic Eruptions by Year *

2013- 83
2010- 82
2009- 67
2008- 78
2007- 71
2006- 76

2005- 73
2004- 71
2003- 64
2002- 67
2001- 64
2000- 67
1999- 66
1998- 56
1997- 52
1996- 59
1995- 58
1994- 58
1993- 58
1992- 57
1991- 64
1990- 55

*USGS data, Volcano Discovery

Surviving a volcanic eruption

Volcanoes are some of nature's most powerful and destructive forces. They unleash tremendous amounts of power, heat, gas, and ash debris. Volcanic eruptions are the way the planet vents or dissipates powerful buildups of heat and magmatic pressure. Volcanic eruptions can come with little warning, and can alter environmental and climate conditions for years. If you live or happen to be residing near what's termed as a 'dormant or sleeping' volcano; you still need to remain alert for any potential signs of unrest from the volcano. 40% of most volcanoes show no prior signs of unrest until the day they erupt. As Earth changes intensify, and the planet succumbs more to a thermal flux, we can expect many more volcanoes to erupt. If you didn't know so-called '*dormant*' volcanoes can suddenly awake with little or no warning, consider these notable volcanic eruptions:

Volcanoes can suddenly wake-up and erupt

- Batu Tara volcano erupted in Indonesia in 2006, after being dormant for 159 years.
- Mount Pinatubo in the Philippines erupted in 1991 in a VEI 6 event, after being dormant for 600 years.
- Chaitén Volcano erupted in 2008 in Chile, after being dormant for 9,500 years.
- Eyjafjallajökull volcano erupted in Iceland in 2010, after being dormant for 180 years.
- Sinabung volcano erupted in Indonesia in 2010, after being dormant for 300 years.
- Nabro volcano erupted in Eritrea in 2011, after never erupting before in the recorded history of 10,000 years.
- Mount Fuji in Japan was stirred by unrest in February of 2012, after being dormant for 300 years.
- Lamongan Volcano in Indonesia began stirring in March of 2012, after 114 years of inactivity.

The Defense

Hazard Threat

Strategy: If you live in the vicinity of a volcano, make preparations well in advance. If you reside in or near the radius of a volcano, you should always be ready for a potential eruption. Volcanoes erupt differently, and the more powerful the eruption is, the farther you will be required by authorities to move away from it. Stock up on emergency necessities. Store at least a three day supply of non-perishable food and portable water at your home. In the event of an eruption, water supplies in your area may become contaminated; so you can't count on a well or public water to drink. If you live in a remote region, fresh water arriving as emergency relief supplies may also be hampered by the devastation or the terrain. Keep a first aid kit, blankets, and warm clothing at your disposal, and have a battery-powered radio and fresh batteries on hand so that you will be able to listen to news advisories if the power goes out. Keep necessary medications together. Ideally, you should keep all these things in one place—a large duffle bag or back pack that you can carry, for example—so that you can bring them with you quickly, if you need to evacuate.

Map out the region: Make a plan and know escape routes in and out of your area- including both main highways and rural roads. In the likelihood of a major eruption, airports would be the first thing to close. Because volcanic ash clogs jet engines, airplanes will not fly into or near ash clouds. If you live near a well-researched and well-monitored volcano, you can probably obtain a hazard zone map from your local emergency management agency, or in the U.S., from the U.S. Geological Survey. In some cases, these volcanic maps can be found online. In the event power is disrupted, you will have to rely on the information contained in this book. Volcanic hazard maps show the probable paths of lava flows and lahars (debris flows) and give estimates for the minimum time it takes for flows to reach a given location. Authorities also generally divide the area around the volcano into zones, from high-risk to low-risk after they set up parameters. Your local emergency agency may also have evacuation routes mapped out. Because volcanic eruptions are dynamic and to some extent, unpredictable, you should have several alternative routes already planned out to reach one or more designated "safe zones."

Know the threat: If you are visiting or hiking near a volcano, knowledge is your most important protection. Bring masks as protection from gassing in the event of an eruption. Respect the power and forces of nature and never venture close to the crater of an active volcano that is emitting gases, steam, or has fumaroles (steam holes). In 1991, husband and wife volcanologist Katia and Maurice Kraft were killed when a violent pyroclastic flow raced down the summit of the Mt. Unzen volcano in Japan and overwhelmed them. No matter what you think you know about a volcano; you are no match for the unpredictable and mercurial forces of nature that can be violently unleashed in a sudden eruption. This advice is doubly apt for crater lakes on an active volcano. Chances are, the waters are already putrid, gaseous, acidic or toxic. Before going to the volcano, consult with local authorities, and heed their recommendations or warnings. Learn about the hazards you may encounter in the area of the volcano, and get a reputable guide to accompany you, if possible. Bring plenty of water in case you become unexpectedly trapped by a lava flow, or fall into a ravine.

Heed evacuation orders: When a volcano erupts, immediately tune into the latest news bulletins or reports from authorities in your area to monitor update status reports on activity at the volcano. If you are in immediate danger or inside a radius of risks; evacuate at once. In November of 2010, over 100 people were killed, many of them were violently burned alive or suffocated, when dense clouds of burning ash descended on villages just 18 km (11 miles) from the volcanic summit of Mount Merapi in Indonesia. The eruption started as a series of rumbles and then progressively worsened. Those who didn't heed the evacuation warnings died instantly. You never know which ejection, in a series of even moderate volcanic eruptions, will be the lethal, powerful one that kills you.

Get to higher ground: Lava flows, lahars, mudflows, and flooding are common in a major eruption, especially if there is heavy rainfall and there is a lot of ash sitting on a mountain or hillsides. All of these can be deadly, and all of them tend to rush down valleys and low-lying areas in downpours. Climb to higher ground, and stay there until you can confirm that the danger has passed. In 1985, the greatest dangers from the eruption of the Nevado del Ruiz volcano in Colombia came from lahars, or mud debris flows. Mudflows raced down the lofty 5,321 meter (17,457 ft) volcanic summit with incredible speed, killing some 23,000 people. The lahars were up to 50 meters thick and six feet deep, and some traveled more than 100 kilometers. Even though the volcanic eruption of Nevado del Ruiz was relatively mild, a VEI 3 event, the death toll from the lahars made it the second deadliest volcanic disaster in the 20th century.

Beware of pyroclastic showers: Sometimes pyroclastic showers of hot, rocky debris actually rain down in some types of eruptions; such as that which occurred at Mount St. Helens in 1980. The ejecta missiles can be blown miles from the volcano's crater. If you ever witness such an eruption shower, protect yourself by staying below the ridgelines of hills, and on the side of the hill opposite the volcano. If you are caught in a hail of smaller pyroclastics, crouch down on the ground, facing away from the volcano, and protect your head with your arms, a backpack, or anything else sturdy that you can find.

Avoid breathing gases or noxious fumes: Volcanoes emit a number of toxic gases, and if you are close enough to one when it erupts, these gases could easily kill you in less than a minute. Breathe through a respirator, mask, or moist piece of cloth—this will also protect your lungs from clouds of ash— and try to get away from the volcano as quickly as possible. Tiny shards of glass in volcanic ash can also lacerate the lungs and cause internal bleeding. Do not stay low to the ground, as some of the most dangerous gases are heavier than air and accumulate near the ground.

Acute respiratory symptoms reported by people in ash fall include:

- Nasal irritation and discharge (runny noses)
- Throat irritation and sore throat, sometimes accompanied by dry coughing
- People with pre-existing chest complaints have developed severe bronchial symptoms which lasted some days beyond exposure to ash (for example, hacking cough, production of sputum, wheezing, or shortness of breath)
- Airway irritation of people with asthma or bronchitis; common complaints of people with asthma include shortness of breath, wheezing, and coughing
- Breathing becomes uncomfortable

Symptoms of eye irritation reported by people in ash fall include:

- Eyes feel as though there are foreign particles in them
- Eyes become painful, itchy or bloodshot
- Sticky discharge or tearing
- Corneal abrasions or scratches
- Acute conjunctivitis or the inflammation of the conjuctival sac that surrounds the eyeball due to the presence of ash,

which leads to redness, burning of the eyes, and photosensitivity

Seek shelter in an ash fall storm: Unless you need to evacuate, the safest place you can be during an eruption and heavy ash fall is inside a strong, sturdy structure. Close all the windows and doors to protect yourself from ash and burning cinders. Beware that heavy ash fall can collect on rooftops and cause them to collapse, especially if the roof is not inclined, and there is heavy rain accompanying an eruption. If you are wounded, burned, or suffering from a respiratory ailment because of the eruption, seek medical attention when it is safe for you to do so.

What you should have in an emergency kit:

- Flashlight and/ or head-band light
- Masks or ventilator
- Water
- A 3 day supply of non-perishable food
- Masking tape to seal doors or cracks
- Eye goggles
- Candles or matches
- Evacuation routes and/ or maps
- Ice scraper to clear your windshield of excess ash
- First-aid kit
- Emergency radio and batteries
- Compass
- Emergency beacons or hazards
- Antenna walking stick to check ash depth if you are outdoors
- Folding shovel if outdoors
- Blanket or thermal insulator
- Backpack

An index of the world's volcanoes

The World's Volcanoes: Where the dangers and stress points are

Mount Adams (Washington, U.S.) - Mount Adams is a potentially active stratovolcano in the Cascade Range and the second-highest mountain in the U.S. state of Washington. The volcano stands at an elevation of 12,281 ft (3,743 m). Adams is a part of the Cascade Volcanic Arc, and is one of the arc's largest volcanoes. It is located in a remote wilderness approximately 31 miles (50 km) east of the Mount St. Helens volcano. The volcano's last noted eruption is believed to have occurred sometime around 550 B.C.

Ambrym Volcano (Vanuatu) - Ambrym is a volcanic island in the archipelago of Vanuatu (formerly known as the New Hebrides). The volcano stands at an elevation of 1,334 m (4,377 ft). It is well known for its highly active volcanic activity that includes lava lake formation. Ambrym is a large basaltic volcano with a 12 km wide caldera. It is considered one of the most active volcanoes of the New Hebrides volcanic arc. The caldera is the result of a huge plinian explosion, which took place around 50 AD. Its explosive force is rated VEI 6, the second highest in the Smithsonian Institution's Volcanic Explosivity Index of the largest volcanic explosions in recent geological history. Ambrym's eruptive activity has been on-going since 2011.

Anak Krakatau Volcano (Indonesia) – Anak is the son of Krakatoa, one of the most destructive volcanoes to ever erupt. Krakatoa's eruption in 1883 was so powerful that it completely disintegrated its volcanic summit, and created the loudest sound ever heard on Earth. Anak

Krakatau sprang up from the ocean in 1927, where its father had once stood 44 years prior. Anak began a series of eruptions on April 2008, and on May 6, 2009. The Volcanological Society of Indonesia put a level orange alert on Anak Krakatau in 2009, and again, in 2011. Anak Krakatau is the fastest growing volcano on Earth-sprouting skyward at an alarming rate of almost 6 meters a year. In March of 2012, scientists found a new lava dome was growing inside the main crater, after the volcano was rattled by 438 tremors in a 24-hour period. Anak is a ticking time bomb waiting to go off.

Arenal Volcano (Costa Rica) - Costa Rica's Arenal volcano erupted in May of 2010, spewing geysers of lava, ash and toxic gases from its crater, and forcing the evacuation of the national park where it is located. The 1,633-metre-tall cone-shaped mountain in northern Costa Rica shuddered into activity at 4 am in the morning; issuing eight successive rivers of lava, which flowed down its steep slopes.

Askja Volcano (Iceland) – Askja volcano is a stratovolcano located in the central region of Iceland. Little was known about the obscure volcano until the volcano exploded in a major eruption on March 29, 1875. In the eastern fjords of Iceland, the ash fall from the eruption was heavy enough to poison the land and kill livestock. As a matter of fact, ash, or tephra, from this eruption was wind-blown as far as Norway and Sweden. The eruption triggered a substantial wave of emigration from Iceland. Another less well-known eruption occurred in the early Holocene circa 11,000 years ago. Tephra from this eruption have been found in southeast Sweden, Northern Ireland, and north Norway. The last eruption of the Askja was in 1961. Geothermal activity has been steadily increasing at the volcano. In June 2010, volcano expert, Hazel Rymer said the growing unrest was probably a sign the volcano would erupt again very soon. In April of 2012, the volcano lake was completely ice-free before the advent of summer; an indication geothermal activity is escalating under the lake. This is a very dangerous volcano. The 1875 eruption was powerful enough to form a large geothermal crater called Víti, which is located on the northeast shore of Öskjuvatn. The crater is approximately 150 meters in diameter. Víti is a geothermal lake of mineral-rich, sulphurous, opaque blue water, which is maintained at a comfortable temperature for swimming. However, the carbon dioxide can also suffocate you in the water on a high emission day and cause you to drown.

Bagana Volcano (Papua New Guinea) - Bagana is an active volcano located in the central part of the island of Bougainville, Papua New Guinea. It is the largest island in the Solomon group. The volcano stands at an elevation of 1,750 m (5,741 ft). It is the most active volcano in the country. Just northeast of Bagana, is the volcano crater lake called Billy Mitchell. It is capable of VEI 5 eruptions. Bagana is one of 17 post-Miocene stratovolcanoes on Bougainville. The volcano is part of the Emperor Range of the Bismarck volcanic arc. On May 16, 2012, NASA satellite images detected a massive lava eruption and plume being expelled from the volcano.

Bárðarbunga Volcano (Iceland) Bárðarbunga, the glacier is a large and powerful stratovolcano, which stands at a height of more than 2,000 meters. It is also Iceland's largest volcanic system, measuring 200 km long and up to 25 km wide. The volcano is submerged in ice, which hides its massive glacier-filled crater. Large volcanic fissure eruptions occur in Iceland about every 5 to 800 years, and this volcano harbors potential dangers of being such an event. The last eruption at Bárðarbunga occurred in 1910, but in December of 2011, the volcano was rattled by a series of small swarms. The largest quake in the swarm series measured ML 3.04 in magnitude and had a depth of 8.5 km. Like many of Iceland's sleeping volcanoes, seismic unrest across the icy landscape appears to be spreading.

Batu Tara Volcano (Indonesia) – Batu Tara is a stratovolcano with has an elevation of about 748 m (2,454 ft). Batu Tara lies on the young and thin oceanic crust, north of the main volcanic Sunda-Banda Arc at the boundary of the collision, between the north moving Australian Plate and the Sunda tectonic plate. In 2006, the volcano erupted for the first time in 159 years. There was notable activity from the volcano again in 2007. On March 26, 2012, Batu Tara emitted a dense ash cloud.

Baekdu Mountain Volcano (North Korea) – Baekdu is an active stratovolcano on the North Korea and China border. The volcano rises to an elevation of 2,744 m (9,003 ft). A large crater lake, called *Heaven Lake* (Korean:천지, Chinese:天池), is in the caldera atop the mountain. The caldera of Baekdu is about 5 km (3.1 mi) wide and 850 m (2,789 ft) deep. The volcano's last notable eruption occurred in 1903. Baekdu is capable of producing a VEI 6 stage eruption and geologists have warned that the volcano could erupt sometime by or before 2020.

Bezymianny Volcano (Russia) – Bezymianny is a stratovolcano that rises to an elevation of 2,882 m (9,455 ft). Bezymianny is the most well-known volcano in Kamchatka, and was once thought extinct. The volcano erupted in 1955, after being dormant for 1,000 years. The eruption was preceded by a failure of a 0.5 sq km section of the volcano. The volcano had a simultaneous eruption with Kamchatka's Klyuchevskaya on January 11, 2010. On March 6, 2012, Bezymianny ejected an 8 km ash cloud.

Bulusan Volcano (Philippines) - Mount Bulusan, or Bulusan Volcano (1,547 m), is the southernmost volcano on Luzon Island, in the Republic of the Philippines. The Bulusan volcano is generally known for its sudden steam-driven or phreatic explosions. It has erupted 15 times since 1885, and is considered to be the 4th most active volcano in the Philippines after Mayon, Taal, and Kanlaon. Bulusan's activity has been on-going since 2011.

Mount Cameroon Volcano (Cameroon) – In early February of 2012, rumbling noises, and tremors accompanied a volcanic explosion at the Cameroon volcano. Prior to the 2012 eruption, the volcano had been relatively quiet, only erupting in 1999 and 2000. Like most of the volcanoes now stirring across the planet, the geologic dynamism for planetary volcanism is slowly morphing.

Campi Flegrei (Italy) - The Phlegraean Fields, also known as Campi Flegrei, (from Greek φλέγος, burning), is a large, 13 kilometer (8.1 mi) wide caldera, situated to the west of Naples, Italy. Campi Flegrei is a supervolcano and any large eruption would devastate most of Europe if the volcano ever unleashed its most destructive forces.

The volcano last erupted in the year 1538. To this day, it remains under very close observation by Italian authorities.

Cerro Machín Volcano (Colombia) - Cerro Machín is a stratovolcano (2,650 m, 8,694 ft) located in the country of Colombia. Cerro Machín is a volcanic plug that is approximately the same age (1,000,000+ years) as the Ruiz-Tolima Massif. The volcano also has the appearance of being part of that same volcanic system. Its sisters are Nevado del Tolima (17,000+ feet), Santa Isabel (15,000 feet), Nevado del Ruiz (17,000+ feet), plus nine other lesser volcanoes, including a 10,000 foot volcanic South Wall containing more than thirty volcanic domes. The volcano had a violent eruption in 1180. On January 15th of 2012, Cerro was shaken by a series of small volcanic tremors.

Chaitén Volcano (Chile) - became active in 2008 after being dormant for 9,500 years. In March of 2010, NASA satellite photography revealed a new dome forming in the Chilean volcano.

El Chichón (Mexico) – The volcano is also called Chichonal (roughly translated in English as "*The bump*"). Chichonal is an active volcano in Francisco León Municipality in northwestern Chiapas, Mexico. Its only known recorded eruptive activity occurred on March 29, April 3, and on April 4, 1982, when it produced a one km-wide caldera that later became an acidic crater lake. A violent eruption followed, which killed around 2,000 people, who lived near the volcano. In the year 2000, the temperature in the volcanic lake began rising again. El Chichón is Mexico's southernmost volcano and is part of the Chiapanecan Volcanic Arc, where subduction of the

Tehuantepec Ridge is occurring on the Cocos Plate, off the Pacific coast of Mexico. In 2012, we noted heightened seismicity in Mexico may be creating potential hazardous scenarios, where some of these volcanoes could reactivate.

Cleveland Volcano (Alaska) - Mount Cleveland is a nearly symmetrical stratovolcano on the western end of Chuginadak Island, which is part of the Islands of Four Mountains, just west of Umnak Island, in the Fox Islands of the Aleutian Islands of Alaska. Mt. Cleveland is 1,730 m (5,676 ft) high, and is one of the most active of the 75 or more volcanoes in the larger Aleutian Arc. Cleveland has erupted at least 21 times in the last 230 years. On December 30, 2011, Cleveland unleashed a 15,000 ft ash cloud. In February of 2012, geologists at the USGS warned Cleveland was in danger of exploding spontaneously due to the large dome that had formed over the crater since its last eruption. On March 7, 2012, the lava dome on Cleveland exploded, in what was described as a significant but 'turbulent explosion.' Activity at the volcano is on-going.

Cotopaxi Volcano (Ecuador) – Cotopaxi is one of the tallest active volcanoes in the world, reaching a height of 5,897 m (19,347 ft). A million people live in Quito, the capitol, just 60 km south of Cotopaxi.

Cumbal Volcano (Colombia) - Cumbal volcano is an active glacier-capped stratovolcano in SW Colombia, located some 25 km SW of the Azufral volcano, and 5.5 km NE of the town of Cumbal - Pueblo. Cumbal is the southernmost active volcano of Colombia that has erupted frequently in historic times. The volcano rises to an elevation of 4,764 m (15,630 ft). A young lava dome occupies the 250 meter wide summit crater, and eruptions from the upper east flank produced a 6 km-long lava field. Thermal springs occur on the SE flanks. The volcano experienced violent eruptions in 1877 and in 1926. In 1988, unrest was reported at the volcano when nearby Geleras began stirring.

Dukono Volcano (Indonesia) - Dukono is an active stratovolcano located on the remote island of Halmahera. The volcano stands at an elevation of 1,185 m (3,888 ft). During a major eruption in the year 1550, a massive lava flow filled in the strait between Halmahera and the north-flank cone of Gunung Mamuya. Many fatalities occurred during the eruption; though the exact number has never been fully known. Dukono is a complex volcano with a broad, low profile, multiple summit peaks and overlapping craters. The volcano erupted in February and May of 2012. Dukono is one of the most active volcanoes in the world.

El Hierro Volcanic Island (Canary Islands) – An earthquake swarm occurred at El Hierro volcano in July 2011 with 720 earthquakes measured in a week. The earthquakes registered between magnitudes 1-3, and most were at a depth of 5-15 km. El Hierro is the youngest of the Canary Islands. On October 10, 2011, an underwater eruption began occurring near La Restinga. The sea began to boil, at times, explosively, and rocks were hurled some 20 meters into the air. In June 2012, the island experienced a seismic swarm and there was deformation of the island by several centimeters.

Eyjafjallajokull Volcano (Iceland) - Iceland's fifth largest sub-glacial volcano registered nearly three thousand quakes between March 2, and March 5, 2010, before it finally erupted on March 20, 2010. In April, a massive ash cloud, ejected by Eyjafjallajokull, suspended all flight traffic across northern Europe. *Magma Plume

Mount Etna (Sicily, Italy) – Etna is the largest volcano in Europe. Etna began erupting in 2007 and 2008 and is still active. In 1992, two streams of lava threatened Zafferana, a municipality inhabited by some 8,000 people. Mt. Etna experienced about 19 major eruptions in 2011 and highly eruptive activity continued in 2012. *Magma Plume

Fernandina Volcano (Galápagos Islands) - Fernandina Island (formerly known in English as Narborough Island, after John Narborough) is the third largest, and youngest, island of the Galápagos Islands. The volcano rises to an elevation of 1,476 m (4,843 ft). The summit caldera of the Fernandina volcano is about 6.5 km (4.0 mi) wide. The Galápagos Islands are an archipelago of volcanic islands, near the equator, in the Pacific Ocean, 972 km (525 mi) west of continental Ecuador; of which they are a part. The volcanic islands, like Hawaii and the Canary Islands, were formed by the Galápagos *hotspot*. The island is an active shield volcano that has been erupting since April 11, 2009. *Magma Plume

Fimmvörðuháls Volcano (Iceland) - Fimmvörðuháls is the area between the glaciers Eyjafjallajökull and Mýrdalsjökull in southern Iceland. The two new craters at Fimmvörduháls were named Magni and Móði (after the sons of Thor, the Norse god of thunder) from an eruption that occurred in 2010. In 2012, this region erupted once again- an indication that pressure near the Katla volcano continues to build. *Magma Plume

Mount Fuji (Japan) – Mount Fuji awakened from its 300 year slumber on February 19, 2012. The last major eruption at the volcano was in 1707. The February 2012 activity included steam eruption from some of its flank vents and volcanic quake swarms. In May of 2012, a team of Japanese researchers discovered a 34 km fault running under the volcano, which, by some estimates, may be capable of producing a 7 magnitude series earthquake. So Fuji has a double set of hazards.

Fuego Volcano (Guatemala) - Rumblings from Fuego shook windows in nearby villages in January of 2012. The volcano is unpredictable and is under constant observation. Its 1974 eruption was monstrous. On November 22, 2011, Fuego unleashed a 2 km ash cloud against a back drop of very loud explosions. In February of 2012, the mercurial volcano erupted again.

Galeras Volcano (Colombia) - Galeras volcano is located in the southern region of Colombia, near the border of Ecuador. The volcanic complex consists of several small calderas, cinder cones, and a stratovolcano. An eruption occurred at the Galeras volcano on January 2, 2010. An ash cloud was ejected from Galeras to a height of 12 km. Hot lava fell 3.5 km from the volcano and started fires. In November of 2011, the volcano was raised to level orange status after harmonic tremors shook the volcano over a 36 hour period.

Gamalama Volcano (Indonesia) – An active stratovolcano (1,715 m or 5,627 ft) located in the Maluku Islands of Indonesia. On December 4, 2011 Mount Gamalama erupted, ejecting material up to 2,000 meters into the air. Thousands of residents in nearby Ternate

City fled due to volcanic ash and dust particles raining down on the town.

Gaua Volcano (Vanuatu) - The picturesque Gaua volcano has erupted 13 times since 1963. In April of 2010, the volcano erupted and forced the evacuation of some 3,000 villagers.

Gorely Volcano (Russia - Kamchatka) – On June 12, 2010, the Gorely volcano expelled an ash cloud several hundred kilometers. The volcano came to life after 20 years of dormancy since its 1980s eruptions.

Mount Galunggung Volcano (West Java, Indonesia) – This 2,168 meter (7,113 ft) stratovolcano is a silent killer. A 1982 (VEI 4) eruption killed 72 people and buried hillsides and villages under meters of mud, lahar, and debris. The last noted eruption occurred in 1984 but in February of 2012, the volcano's alert status was raised after activity increased.

Hekla Volcano (Iceland) – Hekla is an active stratovolcano located in the southern part of Iceland. The volcano rises to an elevation of 1,488 m (4,882 ft). Hekla is one of Iceland's most active volcanoes. More than 20 eruptions have occurred at the volcano since 874 A.D. During the Middle Ages, Europeans called the mercurial volcano the *"Gateway to Hell."* Hekla is part of a volcanic ridge, 40 kilometers (25 mi) long. However, the most active part of this ridge, a fissure about 5.5 km (3.4 mi) long named, Heklugjá, is considered to be the volcano Hekla proper. It is said Hekla looks rather like an overturned boat, with its keel being a series of craters; two of which are generally the most active. The volcano's frequent large eruptions have covered much of Iceland with tephra. These layers have been used to date the eruptions of Iceland's other volcanoes. Hekla's last notable erupted occurred in February of 2000.

Herðubreið Volcano (Iceland) – Herðubreið is a stratovolcano in central Iceland that rises to an elevation of 1,516 m (4,974 ft). Herðubreið volcano, located in the Highlands of Iceland, in the midst of the Ódáðahraun desert, is an isolated, table-mountain shaped broad cone that formed beneath the ice sheet that covered Iceland during the last ice age, which is when the volcano had its last eruption. In May of 2012, the volcano was rattled by a seismic swarm. Like Iceland's many large volcanoes, growing seismic unrest is trickling across the frozen icy landscape.

Hudson Volcano (Chile) –Hudson is a stratovolcano in southern Chile. It is the site of one of the largest eruptions of the 20th century. The mountain itself is covered by a glacier. Hudson stands at about 1,905 m (6,250 ft) in elevation. In October of 2011, the volcano erupted after a series of tremors rattled the region. The Hudson Volcano released three huge columns of steam and ash that combined in a cloud of more than 3 miles in height. An evacuation was ordered for people living in the vicinity of the volcano.

Ijen Volcano (Indonesia) - The Ijen volcano complex is a group of stratovolcanoes in East Java, Indonesia. It is inside a larger caldera Ijen, which is about 20 kilometers wide. The crater sits in a turquoise blue steaming acidic lake which is about 1 km in diameter. The Ijen caldera sits at an elevation of 2,799 m (9,183 ft). On December 17, 2011, the volcano was raised to alert status 2 out of 4 when gas emissions and seismic tremors were attributed to unrest at the volcano. Ijen's last major volcanic eruption occurred in 1999. On March 12, 2012, the volcano was elevated to alert status 3 after thick columns of steam were emitted from the main crater.

Ilaima Volcano (Chile) – At an elevation of 3,125 m (10,253 ft), Ilaima is one of the tallest and most active volcanoes in Chile. It is situated 82 km northeast of Temuco, and 663 km southeast of Santiago, within the borders of Conguillío National Park. The top of the Llaima volcano consists of two summits; the lower of the two, Pichillaima, is about 2,920 m (9,580 ft) high and is significantly less prominent than the higher northern summit. The volcano's last eruption was in 2009. In late March of 2012, the volcano was rattled by a swarm of tremors that tripled in count over a 24 hour period. The volcano was subsequently given a yellow-status alert.

Illiamna Volcano (Aleutian Islands) – According to the AVO, the Alaska Volcano Observatory, there has not been a documented eruption at this volcano in recorded history, yet on January 2012, the volcano began experiencing tremors. On March 9, 2012, the AVO raised the alert level for the volcano after the swarm of tremors intensified. The Illiamana volcano is located on the west side of Cook Inlet, about 135 miles southwest of Anchorage, so any eruption from the volcano would be highly disruptive for the region.

Izalco Volcano (El Salvador) - Izalco is an active stratovolcano on the side of the Santa Ana Volcano, in western El Salvador. The volcano rises to an elevation of 1,950 m (6,398 ft). The Izalco volcano erupted almost continuously from 1770 (when it formed) to 1958, earning it the nickname of *"Lighthouse of the Pacific,"* and it experienced a flank eruption in 1966. During an eruption in 1926, the village of Matazano was buried by ash, killing 56 people.

Kanaga Volcano (Aleutian Islands) – This 9, 840 ft. stratovolcano sprang to life with an ash cloud eruption in February of 2012. This was the first activity from the volcano since 1995. A major eruption and ash cloud from Kanaga could create a flight hazard across the upper portions of North America.

Mount Kanlaon Volcano (Philippines) - is an active volcano on Negros Island in central Philippines. The volcano is 2,168 meters (7,113 ft) in height, and is the most active volcano in central Philippines. The volcano has erupted 26 times since 1886. Eruptions are typically phreatic explosions of the small-to-moderate size variety that produce minor ash-falls near the volcano. In 1902, the volcanic eruption was classified as strombolian in nature, which is typified by the ejection of incandescent cinder, lapilli, and lava bombs. In February of 2012, the volcano's lofty summit was closed after massive cracks were detected near the main crater. Mount Kanlaon's last noted eruption was in 2006.

Karymsky Volcano (Kamchatka) – Karymsky is a stratovolcano on the Kamchatka Peninsula, in Russia, that stands at an elevation of 536 m (5,039 ft). It is the most active volcano of Kamchatka's eastern volcanic zone, a symmetrical stratovolcano constructed within a 5 km wide caldera that formed during the early Holocene period. On March 16, 2012, the volcano emitted a 3,100 meter ash cloud and as a result, the aviation code over the volcano was raised to orange.

Katla Volcano (Iceland) – Katla is one of the largest volcanoes in Iceland. It is situated to the north of Vík í Mýrdal, and to the east of the smaller glacier Eyjafjallajökull. The volcano's peak reaches a height of 1,512 meters (4,961 ft), and is partially covered by the Mýrdalsjökull glacier. The system has an area of 595 km² (230 sq miles). A Katla eruption in Iceland would unleash ten times the explosive power of its little sister, Eyjafjallajokull. In 2010, geologists reported magma was rising in the chamber under Katla. On July 8-9 of 2011, the volcano experienced a small sub-glacial eruption after being flanked with tremors. In January and February of 2012, seismic swarms were frequently reported by MET at the volcano. Katla is capable of producing a VEI 6 stage eruption and she is long overdue for a sizable eruption. Her last major eruption occurred in 1918. ***Magma Plume**

Klyuchevskaya Volcano (Russia) – An eruption occurred on January 11, 2010. The Kamchatka peninsula is one of the most seismically active regions on Earth.

Kīlauea Volcano (Hawaii) – Kileau is a very active shield volcano in the Hawaiian Islands. The volcano stands at an elevation of 1,277 m (4,190 ft). In the early morning hours of March 19, 2008, the volcano experienced its first explosive event since 1924, and the first eruption in the Kīlauea caldera since September 1982. Massive lava flows were reported in 2010. Major eruptions occurred in 2011, and earthquake swarms were reported near the volcano in February of 2012. A new fissure eruption began at the Kilauea volcano on March 5, 2011. The floor of Pu'u O'o crater collapsed over a period of 10 minutes. Activity has been steadily increasing at Kilauea. The fissure ejected lava spatter 20 m high. In 2012, geologists warned the volcano could unleash a very large eruption with little or no warning. *Magma Plume

Kizimen Volcano (Kamchatka) - Kizimen volcano is located in Shchapina graben, on the southeastern edge of the Central Kamchatka Depression. The volcano is similar to Unzen in Japan, in its characteristics. The volcano is capable of producing a VEI 4 stage eruption, similar to Mt. St. Helens. In December of 2011, the volcano unleashed a 7 km ash cloud. The volcano stands at an elevation of 2,376 m (7,795 ft), and as of 2012, it was exhibiting sporadic eruptive volcanic activity. In February of 2012, a large lava flow was detected flowing from the volcano's main crater.

Laacher See Volcano (Germany) – Laacher See is a very large active caldera lake, and a potentially active volcano, in Rhineland-Palatinate, Germany. It is situated close to the cities of Koblenz, about 24 km (15 mi) away, and Bonn, about 37 km (23 mi) away, closest to the towns Andernach, 8 km (5.0 mi), and Mayen 11 km (6.8 mi). The caldera lake lies just 8 km (5.0 mi) from the river Rhine at Andernach. The volcano emits steam and carbon dioxide from the lake. Geologists say the volcano's last eruption probably occurred 12,900 years ago, when it ejected 16 km^3 of tephra in a VEI 6 level event.

La Cumbre Volcano (Galápagos Islands) – La Cumbre is the most active volcano in the Gal Islands. The volcano stands at an elevation of 1,476 m (4,842 feet). The volcano has been erupting since April of 2009, with profuse lava trails flowing into the ocean. The volcano has experienced several collapses of the caldera floor, often following very explosive eruptions. La Cumbre sits over the Galápagos hotspot in the Pacific *Magma Plume

Lamongan Volcano (Indonesia) – Situated in East Java, Indonesia, Lamongan rests at an elevation of 1,651 m (5,417 ft). In March of 2012, the volcano began exhibiting signs of unrest, after remaining relatively quiet since 1898. Increased seismicity and steam seeping from the crater caused authorities in Indonesia to raise the volcano's alert status.

La Palma Volcano (Canary Islands) - Like all of the Canary Islands, La Palma originally formed as a seamount through submarine volcanic activity. La Palma is currently the most volcanically active of the Canary Islands, and was believed to have formed three to four million years ago from a potential magma plume. The base of La Palma lies almost 4,000 meters below sea level and reaches a height of 2,426 meters above sea level. Since the Spanish conquest of the islands in the 15th century, there have been seven major eruptions, with the last occurring in 1971. The volcano is also said to be a tsunami risk for the Atlantic because its summit could possibly collapse and fall into the ocean.

Lascar Volcano (Chile) – Lascar (5,993 meters, 18,346 ft) is the most active stratovolcano of the Chilean Andes. The 1993 eruption deposited ash as far away as Buenos Aires. The volcano's last eruption occurred in 2007. On January 6, 2012, the volcano was placed on heightened alert status after experiencing more than 300 tremors over a 26 hour period.

Lewotolo Volcano (Indonesia) – Lewotolo is a stratovolcano located in the Lesser Sunda Islands of

Indonesia. The volcano (1,423 m, 4,669 ft) is known for explosive eruptive events at the crater. The last noted eruption occurred in 1951. On January 5, 2012, 500 people were evacuated from the vicinity of the volcano after scientists recorded evidence of growing seismic unrest.

Lopevi Volcano (Vanuatu) – Lopevi is an active stratovolcano located in the South Pacific island nation of Vanuatu. The volcano rises to an elevation of 1,413 meters (4,636 ft). The volcano's last notable eruption is said to have occurred in 2008. The volcano is known for both explosive and effusive lava eruptions.

Mount Longonot (Kenya) - Mount Longonot is a large stratovolcano located southeast of Lake Naivasha in the Great Rift Valley of Kenya, Africa. The volcano rises to a height of 2,776 m (9,108 ft). The massive caldera, which is 8 x 12 km large, is believed to have formed by vast eruptions of trachytic lava some 21,000 years ago. Multiple inflation and deflation events are occurring at many of Kenya's volcano, and Longonot was found to have an active magmatic system beneath the caldera. The last noted eruption of the volcano is believed to have occurred in 1863.

Mount Lokon Volcano (Sulawesi, Indonesia) - Mount Lokon is a 1,580 meter (5,184 ft) active stratovolcano in Indonesia. Mount Lokon, together with Mount Empung, forms a twin volcano (2.2 km/1.4 mi apart) in the northern Sulawesi, Indonesia, roughly 10 km (6 mi) south of Manado. The volcano generally harbors a flat and craterless top, so volcanic eruptions are typically quite violent. In July 15, 2011, the volcano erupted with little warning and forced thousands of residents living near its summit to evacuate. On February 10, 2012, the mercurial volcano erupted again, sending an ash cloud racing 2 miles up into the Indonesian sky.

Long Valley Caldera (California) - Long Valley Caldera is a super-volcanic depression in eastern California that is adjacent to Mammoth Mountain. Long Valley is one of the largest calderas on earth, measuring about 20 miles (32 km) long (east-west), and 11 miles (18 km) wide (north-south). The elevation of the floor of the caldera is 6,500 feet (2,000 m) in the east and 8,500 feet (2,600 m) in the west. Seismic swarms occurred at the volcano in 2010 and gases and thermal steam are regularly discharged in regions surrounding the volcano's summit. According to scientists, Long Valley last erupted some 760,000 years ago, and is now over-due for another eruption. A major eruption from a Long Valley supervolcano event would devastate a large southwest region of the U.S. The volcano is closely monitored, but it is enigmatic. Further, its geologic plumbing, especially how the magma chamber is fueled, is not fully understood.

Manam Volcano (Papua New Guinea) - Manam, known locally as Manam Motu, is an island located in the Bismarck Sea, across the Stephan Strait from Yawar on the northeast coast of mainland Papua New Guinea. The volcanic island is 10 kilometers wide, and was created by the activity of the Manam Volcano. Manam is one of the country's most active volcanoes. The volcano rises to an elevation of 1,807 m (5,928 ft). A major eruption of Manam in 1996 killed 13 people. In November 2004, a major eruption from the volcano forced the emergency evacuation of over 9,000 inhabitants of the island.

Manam is very active and activity has been on-going since 2011.

Mount Marapi Volcano (Sumatra, Indonesia) – Mount Marapi is an active stratovolcano in Sumatra that stands about 3,000 meters tall. The volcano erupts frequently. In February of 2012, the volcano unleashed a large ash cloud. More unrest followed. On May 18, 2012, the volcano ejected an ash cloud 600 meters high. The Marapi volcano should not be confused with similarly named, Merapi which is located in Central Java.

Marsili Volcano (Italy) - Marsili is an underwater ticking time bomb located off the coast of Naples, Italy. The volcano is 9,800 feet tall, 44 miles long and 19 miles wide. Volcanologists,with the Italian National Institute of Geophysics and Volcanology (INGV), announced on March 29, 2010, Marsili could erupt any time, as its walls were in the early stages of collapse. An eruption would release vast amounts of magma in an undersea explosion and landslide. Such an event would send a large destructive tsunami careening into Italian coastlines.

Masaya Volcano (Nicaragua) – Masaya (635 m, 2,083 ft) is a circular caldera situated in the Central American Volcanic Belt of Nicaragua. The volcano erupted on October 4, 2003, sending an ash cloud rumbling over the countryside. The volcano regularly emits sulfur dioxide gases, and is continuously smoldering. Its last eruption occurred in 2008. In early January of 2012, vents collapsed on the crater walls, and rumbling noises were reportedly heard at the volcano.

Mayon Volcano (Philippines) - On December 17, 2009, the volcano emitted five ash ejections, with one rising

500 meters above the summit. An Alert level 2 status was declared on the Mayon volcano in June of 2010.

Mount Merapi Volcano (Central Java, Indonesia) – Mount Merapi is a stratovolcano in Central Java. The volcano rises to an elevation of stratovolcano 2,968 m (9,737 ft). Merapi sprang to life with an eruption in 2006 after 12 years of dormancy. Merapi contains an active lava dome which regularly produces pyroclastic flows. The volcano is prone to mercurial fits of violent rage. The October-December 2010 eruptions rained thick ash that killed 353 people and left more than 320,000 homeless. In May of 2012, geologists announced rapid inflation from magma was occurring beneath the volcano's lava dome. The volcano erupted in July of 2012.

Nabro Volcano (Eritrea) - After several 5.7 magnitude earthquakes struck the region of Eritrea, Nabro, a volcano long thought extinct, erupted on June 12, 2011 in a VEI 3-4 stage event. Seven people were killed in the eruption, and the death of 31 others was linked to toxic gas emissions from the volcano's explosive eruption. Dense ash partially covered at least 8 villages in Ethiopia and Eritrea, including Mekele and Asmara. There was also a lava flow 1 km wide and 20 km long. The Nabro volcano is located within the Afar Triangle of the larger Danakil Depression, which harbors many other active volcanoes. The volcano's eruption lingered into 2012. The unexpected Nabro eruption is one more sign the African continent is tearing along the Great Rift Valley.

Nevado del Huila Volcano (Colombia) - The volcano's summit, at 5,364 m above sea level, is the highest in Colombia's Andean Central Cordillera. The crater is capped by ice. On June 16, 2010, the government raised the alert status code from yellow to orange after increased activity was detected at the volcano. Nevado del Huila experienced a short eruption in 2012.

Nevado del Ruiz Volcano (Colombia) - The Nevado del Ruiz (also known as La Mesa de Herveo, or Kumanday in the language of the local pre-Columbian indigenous people), is a stratovolcano located on the border of the departments of Caldas and Tolima in Colombia, about 129 kilometers (80 mi) west of the capital city Bogotá. Nevado del Ruiz, which lies about 129 kilometers (80 mi) west of Bogotá, is part of the Andes mountain range. The volcano is part of the Ruiz–Tolima volcanic massif (or Cordillera Central), a group of five ice-capped volcanoes which includes: the Tolima, Santa Isabel, Quindio and Machin volcanoes. Nevado lies in the Northern Volcanic Zone of the Andean Volcanic Belt. On November 13, 1985, a small eruption from Nevado del Ruiz produced an enormous lahar (volcanic mud and debris flow) that buried and destroyed the town of Armero in Tolima; causing an estimated 25,000 deaths. Nevado's danger comes from its lofty elevation. Though the volcano is only 2,035 meters (6,677 feet) in height; it sits at an elevation of about 17,457 feet- making any debris flows racing down its slopes extremely dangerous. The 1985 Nevado lahar event later became known as the Armero tragedy. It was the deadliest lahar eruption in recorded history. An estimated 500,000 people live near the volcano and could be in danger from an eruption. Nevado's last major eruption occurred in 1994. On February 23, 2012, an increase in seismic activity was reported at the volcano. The unrest was marked by shallow earthquakes, associated with magmatic fluid movements, and the fracturing of rock. Geologists also measured increased

SO$_2$ emissions, and there were some changes in strain measurements. On March 9, 2012, geologists in Colombia warned that the sleeping volcano was awakening. On March 12, 2012, Nevado del Ruiz erupted, emitting thick columns of ash and smoke. Towns, within the vicinity of the volcano, were alerted to potential dangers.

Ngauruhoe Volcano (New Zealand) - Mount Ngauruhoe is an active stratovolcano, or composite cone in New Zealand. The cone is made from layers of lava and tephra. The volcano rises to an elevation of 2,291 m (7,516 ft), and overlooks the Rangipo Desert. It is the youngest vent in the Tongariro volcanic complex on the Central Plateau of the North Island. The volcano's first eruption occurred 2,500 years ago. Subsequently, the volcano has erupted no less than twenty times during the 20th century. The volcano became the fictional *'Mount Doom'* in the New Line *Lord of the Rings* film series. Ngauruhoe's last eruption was said to have occurred in 1977.

Novarupta Volcano (Alaska) - Novarupta, meaning *"new eruption,"* is a relatively new volcano. It is located on the Alaskan Peninsula in Katmai National Park and Preserve, about 290 miles (470 km) southwest of Anchorage. The volcano rises to an elevation of 841 meters (2,759 ft). The volcano formed in 1912, during the largest volcanic eruption of the 20th century, besides Mount Pinatubo in 1991. Novarupta released 30 times the volume of magma as the 1980 eruption of Mount St. Helens. At nearby Kodiak, the ash was so thick, that two days following the eruption, local residents could not see a lantern held at arm's length. The Novarupta eruption was rated a VEI 6 event in terms of the explosive nature of the eruption.

Nyiragongo Volcano (Congo) – Nyiragongo, and nearby Nyamuragira are together responsible for 40% of Africa's historical volcanic eruptions. The main crater of Nyiragongo is about two km wide and usually contains a lava lake. In 2002, lava from an eruption reached the city of Goma, where at least 15% of the buildings were destroyed. The eruption left more than 120,000 homeless and killed 45. The volcano erupted in dramatic fashion again in November of 2011. In January of 2012, the volcano exploded, ejecting lava fountains 50-150 meters high, and sent lava bombs as high as 600 meters.

Ol Doinyo Lengai Volcano (Tanzania) - after fostering 6.0 tremors, the volcano erupted on September 4, 2007. The volcano's name means the *"Mountain of God."* Lengai experienced volcanic tremors on April 25, 2010 after an earthquake shook Tanzania and awakened the 2,900 meter sleeping giant.

Pacaya Volcano (Guatemala) – Pacaya is an active volcano complex in Guatemala. It is believed to have first erupted some 23,000 years ago. Subsequently, it has erupted at least 23 times since the Spanish conquest of Guatemala. Pacaya rises to an elevation of 2,552 meters (8,373 ft). Pacaya is one of the world's oldest active volcanoes. It erupted in 2010, emitting a dense cloud of steam and gas.

Pagan Volcano (Mariana Islands) – North Pagan is the more active of the two stratovolcanoes on Pagan Island. The volcano rises to an elevation of 570 m (1,870 ft). Mount Pagan is a stratovolcano that saw its most dramatic eruption in 1981. In 2012, the volcano on the remote island erupted again.

Pago Volcano (New Britain, Papua New Guinea) – Pago is an active stratovolcano complex located in the New Britain region of Papua New Guinea, east of Kimbe. Pago is a young post-caldera cone within the Witori caldera. The Buru caldera cuts the SW flank of the Witori volcano. Pago has a very violent past and the volcano is capable of VEI 6 level eruptions. In May of 2012, the volcano erupted and emitted a plume of ash up to an elevation of 13.7 km (45,000 feet).

Mount Pelée Volcano (Martinique) – Pelée is an active volcano at the northern end of the island of Martinique, in the Lesser Antilles island arc of the Caribbean. The volcano rises to an elevation of 1,397 meters (4,583 ft). Pelée's volcanic cone is composed of layers of volcanic ash and hardened lava. The stratovolcano is famous for its eruption in 1902, which has been dubbed by scientists as the worst volcanic disaster of the 20th century. The violent eruption of Pelée killed about 30,000 people. Most of the deaths were the results of pyroclastic flows, which rumbled down the summit and engulfed the city of Saint-Pierre, the largest city on the island. Pyroclastic flows completely destroyed St. Pierre, a town of 30,000 people, within minutes of the eruption. The eruption left only two survivors in the direct path of the volcano (with a third reported to have narrowly escaped before the city was engulfed by lava): Louis-Auguste Cyparis survived because he was in a poorly ventilated, dungeon jail cell; Léon Compère-Léandre, another resident living on the edge of the city, escaped with severe burns. Havivra Da Ifrile, a young girl, reportedly escaped with injuries during the eruption, by taking a small boat to a cave down shore. She was later found unconscious in a boat adrift two miles (3 km) from the island. The volcano erupted again in 1929, and as recent as 2010, fumaroles were reported simmering from the main crater.

Mount Pinatubo (Philippines) - Mount Pinatubo is an active stratovolcano located on the island of Luzon, near the tri-point of the Philippine provinces of Zambales, Tarlac, and Pampanga. The volcano stands at a height of 1,485 m (4,872 ft). It is about 300 meters shorter since the eruption of 1991. Pinatubo is part of the Cabusilan Mountains separating the west coast of Luzon from the central plains. Before the volcanic eruption of 1991, the volcano's eruptive history was relatively unknown, so few suspected the degree of danger unleashed by Pinatubo's powerful VEI 6 eruption. Prior to the eruption, the volcano's summit was also heavily eroded, inconspicuous, and obscured from view. It was covered with dense forest which supported a population of several thousand indigenous people- the Aetas, who fled to the mountains during the Spanish conquest of the Philippines. The volcano's Plinian /Ultra-Plinian eruption on June 15, 1991 produced the second largest terrestrial volcanic eruption of the 20th century. Only the eruption of Novarupta, in the Alaska Peninsula, in 1912 was more powerful.

Poás Volcano (Costa Rica) - The Poás volcano rises to an elevation of 2,708 m (8,885 ft). The volcano has periodically erupted about 39 times since 1828. Poás was near the epicenter of a 6.1-magnitude earthquake in January 2009 that killed at least forty people. The volcano experienced eruptive activity in 2009, involving minor phreatic eruptions and landslides within the northern active crater. Poás eruptions often include geyser-like ejections of crater lake water. The volcano experienced another explosive eruption in 2011. In February of 2012, park rangers reported strong high-temperature fumarolic activity and sporadic small phreatic explosions in the main crater.

Popocatepetl Volcano (Mexico) - Rising to a height of 5,400 (17,800 ft) above sea level, the eruption of the volcano dubbed *"the Smoking Mountain"* could be a serious threat to some 9 million people in Mexico City, as well as towns and villages located within vicinity of the volcano. Popocatepetl is one of the most violent volcanoes in Mexico. The volcano has been shaken by no less than 20 huge eruptions since the 16th century. In 2000, thousands of people were evacuated just before Popocatepetl exploded and caused enormous glacial melting. With Mexico City sinking lower into the Earth, a major eruption of Popocatepetl could be something almost apocalyptic. In 2012, a series of major, large earthquakes began tearing at the western coastline of Mexico. On January 25, 2012, Popocatepetl erupted after rumbling for several days. Unrest at one of Mexico's most dangerous volcanoes continues to grow. In April of 2012, major alerts were posted by local officials when the volcano threatened to erupt again.

Piton de la Fournaise (Reunion Island) – The name means *"Peak of the Furnace."* Piton is a shield volcano on the eastern side of Réunion Island in the Indian Ocean. The volcano's elevation is 2,632 m (8,635 ft). The volcano's last noted eruption was in January of 2010.

Putana Volcano (Bolivia-Chile) Putana is an active stratovolcano located on the border of Chile and Bolivia. The volcano's lofty elevation rises to some 5,890 m (19,324 ft). Strong fumarolic activity is present at the summit crater, and is visible from a great distance. The volcano has large sulfur deposits. The volcano, whose name literally means *"whore,"* is believed to have erupted twice in historic times. Putana is simmering and may prove in the long run that she is nothing to be trifled with.

Puyehue-Cordón Caulle (Chile) – The volcanic complex is composed of two coalesced volcanic edifices which form a major mountain massif in the Puyehue National Park of the Andes of Ranco Province, Chile. The complex stands at an elevation of about 2,236 meters (7,336 feet). After a series of tremors, on June 4, 2011, the volcanic complex erupted in a VEI 3 stage event. The ash cloud drifted over three countries in South America and led to the evacuation of thousands of people. Millions of head of livestock perished in the dense ash cloud. The eruption of the volcano lingered into 2012.

Quetzaltepec Volcano (San Salvador) - See San Salvador Volcano.

Mount Rainer Volcano (Washington) - Mount Rainier is an active volcano believed to have erupted 500,000 years ago. It is considered one of the most dangerous volcanoes on Earth because of its tremendous height, and the potential threat posed by summit avalanches, and lahar in a debris flow, should it ever erupt. Because of Rainier's lofty elevation (14,410 feet above sea level) and northerly location, glaciers have cut deep into its lavas, making it appear deceptively older than it actually is. Mount Rainier is known to have erupted as recently as the 1840s, and large eruptions took place as recently as 1,000 to 2,300 years ago. Mount Rainier and other similar volcanoes in the Cascade Range, such as Mount

Adams, and Mount Baker, erupt much less frequently than the more familiar Hawaiian volcanoes. However, their eruptions are vastly more destructive. Hot lava and rock debris from Rainier's eruptions have melted snow and glacier ice, and triggered debris flows (mudflows) with a consistency of churning wet concrete. These debris flows have swept down all river valleys radiating from the volcano. Debris flows have also been spawned by the collapse of unstable parts of the volcano without any accompanying eruptions. Some debris flows have traveled as far as the present margin of Puget Sound. Much of the lowland to the east of Tacoma and the south of Seattle was formed by pre-historic debris flows from Mount Rainier. [1]

Raoul Island Volcano (New Zealand) Raoul is the largest and northernmost of the main Kermadec Islands. The volcano rises to an elevation of 516 m (1,693 ft). Raoul has experienced violent, vigorous eruptions over the last several thousand years. The volcano's last noted eruption occurred in 2006. Growing seismic and submarine volcanic unrest along the Tonga –Kermadec volcanic arc could increase unrest for Raoul.

Mount Redoubt Volcano (Alaska) - Mount Redoubt, or Redoubt Volcano, is an active stratovolcano in the dense volcanic Aleutian Range of the U.S. state of Alaska. The volcano rises to an elevation of 10,197 ft (3,108 m). The volcano sprang to life in 2009, after being asleep for 20 years. Redoubt experienced an earthquake swarm in 2010 and remains under close observation.

Reventador Volcano (Ecuador) Reventador is an active stratovolcano in the eastern Andes of Ecuador. The volcano is located in a remote area of the national park of the same name. Since 1541, the volcano has erupted over 25 times, although its isolated location means that many of its sporadic eruptions have gone relatively unreported. Reventador's last major eruption occurred in 2009, but the largest historical eruption of the volcano happened in 2002. During the 2002 eruption, ash plumes from the volcano reached heights of 17 km, and pyroclastic flows fanned out 7 km from the cone. In 2012, the volcanoes in the Andes of Ecuador started rumbling. In February of 2012, lava reportedly oozed from Reventador's crater.

Rincón de la Vieja (Costa Rica) – Rincón is an active andesitic complex volcano in NW Costa Rica. The volcano rises to an elevation of 1,916 m (6,286 ft). The volcano erupted in 2011, and in May of 2012, Rincón was placed on raised alert status after reported renewed activity.

Rinjani Volcano (Indonesia) – Mount Rinjani is an active stratovolcano on the island of Lombok. The volcano rises to an elevation of 3,726 m (12,224 ft). Rinjani expelled a 4,000 ft ash cloud in May of 2010.

Mount Ruapehu Volcano (New Zealand) - Mount Ruapehu, or just Ruapehu, is an active stratovolcano at the southern end of the Taupo Volcanic Zone in New Zealand. The volcano rises to an elevation of 2,797 m (9,177 ft). Ruapehu last erupted in September of 2007, when a hydrothermal steam emission erupted from a vent near the main crater. The 2007 eruption came with no warning. Since 2007, the volcano has been under heightened alert levels after activity increased both in 2008, and 2011. To this day, the New Zealand volcano remains relatively unpredictable.

Mount St. Helens (Washington, U.S.) - Mount St. Helens is an active stratovolcano located in Skamania County, in the Pacific Northwest region of the United States. Mount St. Helens is part of the Cascadian volcanic mountain range. The volcano rises to an elevation of 8,365 ft (2,550 m), and is located 96 miles (154 km) south of Seattle, and 50 miles (80 km) northeast of Portland, Oregon. On March 20, 1980, Mount St. Helens was shaken by a magnitude 4.2 earthquake, which awakened the volcano from slumber. Seven days later, on March 27, 1980, the volcano began venting steam. By the end of April, the north side of the mountain began to bulge. On May 18, 1980, a second 5.1 earthquake hit the mountain, triggering a massive explosion, and the collapse of the northern summit. The eruption came with little or almost no warning. The St. Helens May 18 eruption released 24 megatons of thermal energy. It also ejected more than 0.67 cubic miles (2.79 km3) of material in a VEI 5 event. The collapse of the north side of the mountain reduced St. Helens' height significantly by 1,300 feet (400 m) and left a crater 1 mile (1.6 km) to 2 miles (3.2 km) wide and 0.5 miles (800 m) deep in a huge breach. Since the 1980 eruption, a lava dome has formed in the crater and periodic emissions of steam were noted between 2004 and 2008. Any volcano that can be so easily awakened by an earthquake is dangerous. One that sits in a powerful subduction zone that is long overdue for a major earthquake is even more unsettling.

Sangay Volcano (Ecuador) - Sangay is an active stratovolcano located in central Ecuador. Sangay is the southernmost volcano in the Northern Volcanic Zone. It is the most active volcano in Ecuador. The volcano rises to an elevation of 5,230 m (17,159 ft). It has only erupted three times in recorded history; exhibiting mostly strombolian activity. Since the 23rd of January 2012, there has been a steady intensification of activity at the Sangay volcano, as indicated by pilots who reported the presence of ash drifting from the volcano.

San Pedro-Pellado Volcano (Chile) - The San Pedro-Pellado volcanic complex (also known as San Pedro-Tatara) has been active from the Pliocene to the Holocene era. The summit elevation rises to 3,621 m (11,880 feet). In June of 2012, authorities in Chile reported an earthquake swarm at the volcano. Any eruption of the volcano would be the first in recorded history.

San Salvador Volcano (San Salvador) – The San Salvador volcano is also known as Quetzaltepec. San Salvador is a stratovolcano that is located northwest of the city of San Salvador. The volcano's elevation is 1,893 m (6,211 ft). The 6 km crater has been filled with a relatively newer edifice, the Boquerón volcano. The volcano last erupted in 1917. About 540,000 people live in the city of San Salvador. A potential eruption would pose some threat to those living in the vicinity of the volcano's summit. The volcano had been asleep until six earthquakes struck the volcano on the morning of March 21, 2012- one day after a strong 7.4 magnitude earthquake rattled Oaxaca, Mexico. An evacuation was ordered by Civil defense services, due to the rise in seismic activity at the volcano on March 22, 2012. The volcano remains under close observation.

Santa Maria Volcano (Guatemala) – Santa María Volcano is a large active volcano in the Western Highlands of Guatemala, which is close to the city of

Quetzaltenango. Its eruption in 1902 (VEI 6), was one of the four largest eruptions of the 20th century. It has been said that Santa María's eruption was probably one of the largest eruptions seen on the planet in the last 200 years. The volcano rises to an elevation of 3,772 m (12,375 ft), and is part of the Sierra Madre range of volcanoes. They extend along the western edge of Guatemala and are separated from the Pacific Ocean by a broad plain. The volcano sprang to life again in 2009. In May of 2010, Santa Maria (also known as *Santiaguito*) expelled a column of ash and debris 27,000 feet into the air. In January of 2012, Santa Maria expelled ash clouds of 800 meters. In February of 2012, the volcano was shaken by a violent spasm of eruptions, which emitted volcanic debris every 15 minutes. In March of 2012, the volcano was rattled by thirty-tree explosions. Santa Maria is a mercurial and very dangerous volcano.

Santorini Volcano (Greece) - The Greek island is the site of one of the largest volcanic eruptions in recorded history. The Minoan eruption (also known as the Thera eruption), is believed to have occurred some 3,600 years ago at the height of the Minoan civilization. The eruption left a large caldera surrounded by volcanic ash deposits hundreds of feet deep. Some scholars theorize the eruption led indirectly to the collapse of the Minoan civilization when the island of Crete, 110 km (68 mi) to the south, was inundated by a gigantic tsunami. Santorini Island is the remnant of a volcanic cone, whose top was blown off by an inconceivable amount of violent geological force. The scale of the super-colossal volcanic eruption was believed to be in the range of VEI 7, the highest next to a super-volcanic eruption. On January 27, 2012, the idyllic island of Crete was rattled by two 5.2

magnitude earthquakes. Subsequent earthquake swarms were detected near the Santorini caldera. The monster volcano of Greece could be waking up. In March of 2012, Georgia Tech Associate Professor Andrew Newman, who has studied Santorini since setting up more than 20 GPS stations on the island in 2006, said the volcano was awake, and inflating at a rate of between five and nine centimeters laterally. Newman told the BBC that the chamber had expanded by 14 million cubic meters since January of 2012.

Semeru Volcano (Indonesia) – Semeru is an active stratovolcano that measures some 3,676 meters (12,060 ft) in height. Sermeru is the highest summit on the island of Java. Semeru's history is replete with eruptions. Since 1818, at least 55 eruptions have been recorded (10 of which, resulted in fatalities), consisting of both lava flows and pyroclastic flows. All historical eruptions have been a VEI of 2 or 3. On February 6, 2012, the alert level status on Semeru was raised to alert status level 3 out of 4, after an increase in activity was noted at the volcano.

Mount Shasta Volcano (California) - Mount Shasta is not connected to any nearby mountain and dominates the northeastern Californian landscape. The volcano rises abruptly and stands nearly 10,000 feet (3,000 m) above the surrounding terrain. Mt. Shasta is part of the Cascade Mountain Range. Since the Holocene period, Mount Shasta has erupted about every 800 years. The last eruption occurred in 1786. There are fumaroles on the volcano's mountainside, indicating the volcano is still very much alive, though the USGS lists it as dormant.

Shiveluch Volcano (Russia – Kamchatka) Shiveluch is one of Kamchatka's largest and most active volcanoes.

Shiveluch rises to an elevation of 3,307 m (10,850 ft). Shiveluch began forming about 60,000 to 70,000 years ago, and has had at least 60 large eruptions during the Holocene period. On June 17, 2010, Russia's northern most active volcano expelled an ash cloud to a height of 4,000 meters (13,000 feet). A second ash cloud of 6.5 km erupted from the volcano on June 24, 2010. In February of 2012, a lava flow was detected erupting from the vicinity of a crater formed in 2010.

Mount Sirung Volcano (Indonesia) – Mount Sirung, also known as *Gunung Sirung,* is an active volcano complex located on Pantar Island in the Alor archipelago of the eastern Indonesian province of Nusa Tenggara Timor. The volcano rises to an elevation of 862 m (2,828 ft), and is known for its potent gas emissions. The crater rim of the volcano can be reached by an easy hike from the village of Kakamauta. A large sulphurous lake and several active fumaroles churn inside the crater. The volcano's last noted eruption occurred in 1970, and regular gas and clastic eruptions have occurred since 2004. On May 13, 2012, the volcano erupted again forcing some 250 people from the Mauta village on its slope, to seek safety elsewhere in the district. People fleeing the May 2012 eruption complained of various respiratory ailments, as a result of the ash and toxic gas inhalations emanating from the volcano.

Soufrière Hills volcano (Montserrat) – The volcano erupted violently on February 10, 2010, and propelled pyroclastic flows down several sides of the mountain. The word *'Soufrière'* means *'sulfur'* in French. On February 11, 2010, the volcano expelled a massive ash cloud 40,000 feet into the air. In March of 2012, the volcano experienced a surprise eruption with the ejection of a pyroclastic flow which traveled about 1 km to the west towards Plymouth, before drifting out to sea. Montserrat Volcano Observatory said at the time of the eruption: "There were no precursors to that event. Although activity has generally been low, this event clearly illustrates that the Soufrière Hills Volcano is still an active volcano system and that pyroclastic flows can occur at any time with little to no warning." [2]

Soputon Volcano (Indonesia) – Soputon is an active stratovolcano on the southern rim of the Quaternary Tondano caldera, on the northern arm of Sulawesi Island. It is one of Sulawesi's most active volcanoes. The volcano rises to an elevation of 1,784 m (5,853 ft). Soputon had a strong eruption in 2011, and in 2012 the alert level was raised on the volcano in May, after very strong activity was reported by local officials.

Stromboli Volcano (Sicily) – Stromboli is a small island in the Tyrrhenian Sea, off the north coast of Sicily, containing one of the three active volcanoes in Italy. Stormboli is one of the eight Aeolian Islands which comprise a volcanic arc north of Sicily. Stromboli began erupting in 2000 with the formation of two new craters. Stromboli began showing signs of activity in 2010 and eruptions at the volcano are currently ongoing.

Sakurajima Volcano (Japan) - Sakurajima erupted after years of being dormant, sending debris up to 2 km high on March 10, 2009. Sakurjima is currently one of the most active volcanoes in the world. Kagoshima city, a population of half a million, is located 10 km west of Sakurajima Volcano. Sakurajima has been called the Vesuvius of the East. The number of eruptions at

Sakurajima in 2010 doubled the number reported in 2009. Some volcanologists feel the volcano is being pushed to the point of a new catastrophe. The volcano's violent, explosive activity is continuous, and it remains a mercurial volatile time bomb. On March 12, 2012, Sakurajima unleashed the largest explosive eruption seen on the summit in three years.

Suwanose-Jima Volcano (Ryukyu Islands, Japan) - Suwanose-jima is a volcanic island with a population of about 50 people. The volcano is 8 km long and is one of the most active in Japan. The volcano rises to an elevation of 799 m (2,621 ft). Suwanose-jima experienced a moderate eruption on July 6, 2009. A magnitude 6.9 earthquake occurred 55 km SE of Suwanose-jima volcano on October 30, 2009. A 7.1 earthquake also struck near the volcano on February 26, 2010. This volcano may be on a seismic ignition switch.

Taal Volcano (Philippines) – Taal Volcano is a complex volcano located on the island of Luzon, in the Philippines. Historical eruptions are concentrated on Volcano Island, an island near the middle of Lake Taal. The volcano rises to an elevation of 400 m (1,312 ft). Taal is another Ring of Fire volcano with a rich history of violent eruptions. On June 8, 2010, scientists reported Taal was undergoing a magmatic intrusion, which suggests an eruption will eventually happen. The whole Taal Volcano Island is a high-risk area and a Permanent Danger Zone (PDZ). Permanent settlements within vicinity of the volcano are strictly prohibited. In June of 2010, Taal was raised to Alert Level 2. On May 28, 2011, Taal was shaken by a series of earthquake swarms. The pronounced volcanic activity lasted until June and included CO_2 gas emissions, a fish kill, and churning from the crater lake. Taal last erupted in 1977 and the volcano may be overdue for more activity.

Mount Tambora Volcano (Indonesia) – Mount Tambora is a stratovolcano on the island of Sumbawa. The volcano rises to an elevation of 2,722 m (8,930 ft). With an estimated ejecta volume of 160 km³ (38 cu mi) tephra, Tambora's 1815 outburst was the largest volcanic eruption known in recorded history. The explosion was reportedly heard on Sumatra Island more than 2,000 km (1,200 mi) away. The eruption was ranked as a VEI 7 event which killed some 71,000 people. The violent 1815 eruption ejected so much volcanic ash and debris into the atmosphere, that it altered global climate conditions across the planet. The year 1816 was known as *'the year without a summer.'* Mount Tambora is still active. Minor lava domes and flows have extruded from the caldera floor during the 19th and 20th centuries. The last eruption of Tambora occurred in 1967.

Mount Tarawera Volcano (New Zealand) – The Mount Tarawera volcano is responsible for both New Zealand's largest dome volcanic eruption, and largest historic eruption. The volcano rises to an elevation of 1,111 m (3,645 ft) and is located 24 kilometers southeast of Rotorua in the North Island. It consists of a series of rhyolitic lava domes that were fissured down the middle by an explosive basaltic eruption in 1886 that killed over a hundred people. The 1886 eruption came as a surprise to natives who thought the volcano was dormant. Future eruptions may be equally enigmatic and unpredictable.

Tungurahua Volcano (Ecuador) In May of 2010, the volcano expelled a 7 km high ash plume, which created a rolling ash cloud. The dense cloud of debris blanketed towns in the vicinity of the volcano with ash. The sound of the eruption was so loud; it was heard in the towns of Banos and Guadalupe, some 14 km away. In November of 2011, Tungurahua unleashed pyroclastic boulder flows which roared down its rocky summit, even as deep explosive rumbling noises shook residents' windows up to 14 km (8.6 miles) away from the volcano. Tungurahua rises to an elevation of 5,023 meters (16,480 ft), and its elevation makes it very dangerous for debris flows. On March 4, 2012, the volcano was rocked by strombolian eruptions following four loud explosions. On March 20, 2012, the volcano convulsed again with explosions that were heard at a distance of 14 km from the volcano.

Turrialba and Poás Volcanoes (Costa Rica) Turrailba is a stratovolcano that rises to an elevation of 3,340 m (10,958 ft) high. The summit has three craters which are composed of fumaroles and sulfur pits. Huge columns of gas and steam erupted from the twin volcanoes on April 26, 2010. On January 27, 2012, Costa Rica's Turrialba volcano produced a burst of activity that shot water vapor and ash more than 15,000 feet into the air. In March of 2012, two large gas and steam emission were reportedly expelled from the main crater. In May of 2012, authorities raised the threat level on Turrialba to yellow after temperatures inside the crater precipitously rose to an astounding 800° Celsius.

Ulawun Volcano (Papua New Guinea) – Ulawun is one of the most active and dangerous volcanoes in Papua New Guinea. Ulawun is the highest volcano in the 1,000 km long Bismarck volcanic arc, which stretches from Rabaul to Wewak. Ulawun volcano is composed of lava flows interblended with tephra, composed of basalt and andesite. Several thousand people live within vicinity of the volcano. There have been 22 recorded eruptions at Ulawun since the 18th century. Major ash emissions were reported on February 14, 2010, and again in 2011.

Uturuncu supervolcano (Bolivia) - Uturuncu, a 6,008 m (19,711 ft) volcano located in southwestern Bolivia, is expanding at a rate of between one to two centimeters per year. The volcano is "inflating with astonishing speed," reports *OurAmazingPlanet*'s Andrea Mustain. The land rising around Uturuncu is about 70 km wide. Magma is inflating the underground chambers of the caldera at the fastest rate known on Earth. At the rate Uturuncu is uplifting; scientists estimate the magma beneath the caldera is expanding by 27 cubic feet every second. Scientists do not know what the rapid uplift signifies, however, they do agree the growth of the volcano is attributable to magma intrusion at depths which imply that a large reservoir of magma is coalescing under Uturuncu. Fumaroles are active near the summit. There is no doubt that Uturuncu may represent a new breed of supervolcano.

Mount Vesuvius (Italy) - Mount Vesuvius remains one of the world's most dangerous volcanoes. The volcano has an eruption cycle of about every 20 years. The last eruption of Vesuvius occurred in 1944, so the volcano is considered long overdue. The volcano is rated as one of the most dangerous in the world because millions of people live within close proximity to the summit. It must not be forgotten that the famed 79 A.D. eruption, which obliterated Pompeii and Herculaneum, came with little or no warning.

Yasur Volcano (Vanuatu) – Mount Yasur is an active volcano on Tanna Island, Vanuatu. Yasur rises to an elevation of 361 m (1,184 ft). Some activity was reported at the volcano in May of 2009, but Yasur's violent Strombolian explosions in June of 2010 may be cause for future concerns about the volcano. In 2011, Yasur erupted again and subsequently, activity at the volcano has been ongoing and continuous.

Yellowstone supervolcano (U.S.) - A swarm began at the world's most dangerous sleeping super volcano on January 17, 2010 that by February 11, 2010, had seen more than 1,805 earthquakes. Geologists believe Yellowstone's last major eruption occurred 640,000 years ago and the volcano is long overdue for a major eruption.

Indonesian Volcanoes- On March 17, 2010, 18 of Indonesia's volcanoes were put on alert status level 2, after they began emitting toxic gases and fumes. Indonesia has 129 volcanoes.

Japanese Volcanoes- Japan has about 121 active volcanoes, and it was feared as many as 22 were activated by the March 11, 2011, 9.0 magnitude earthquake that struck near Honshu Japan.

Volcanic hazard maps

Volcanic hazards Northwest U.S. – Cascade Range

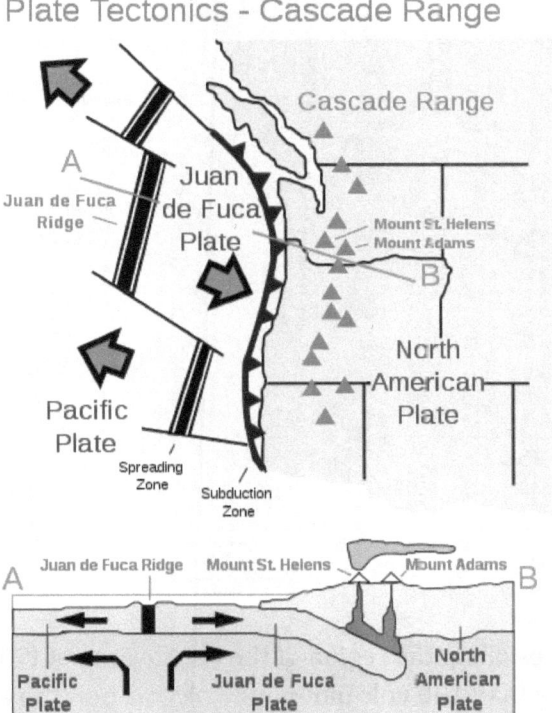

The Cascade Volcanoes (also known as the Cascade Volcanic Arc or the Cascade Arc) are a number of volcanoes in a volcanic arc, in western North America, extending from southwestern British Columbia through Washington; and Oregon to Northern California, in a distance of well over 700 mi (1,100 km). The volcanic arc was formed due to subduction along the Cascadia subduction zone.

*Map courtesy of USGS

151

Volcanic hazards Alaska

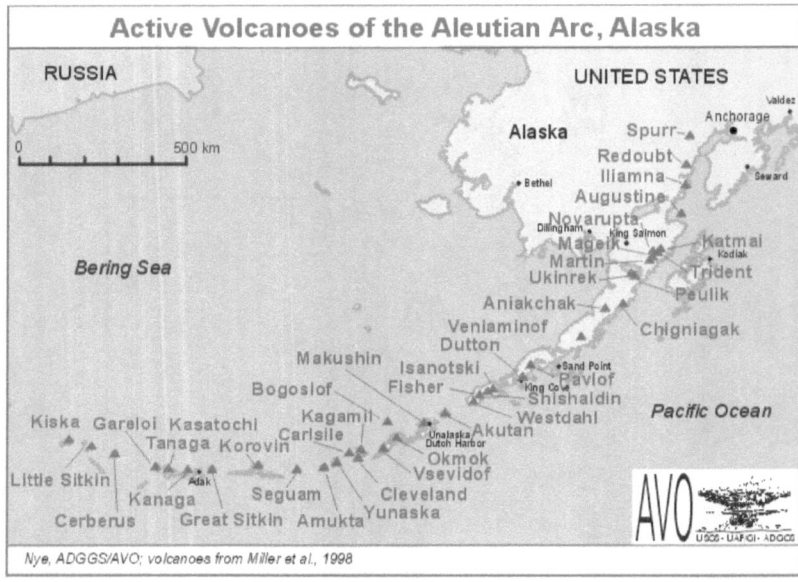

Active Volcanoes of the Aleutian Arc, Alaska

Nye, ADGGS/AVO; volcanoes from Miller et al., 1998

Alaska lies along the region of the Pacific Ring of Fire. There are more than 100 volcanoes and volcanic fields in Alaska. More than 40 of Alaska's volcanoes have been active in historic times. These volcanic "hotspots" make up 80 percent of all of the active volcanoes in the U.S., and 8 percent of all active above water volcanoes on earth. Most, or all, of Alaska's volcanoes are located along the 1,500 mile Aleutian Arc that extends westward to Kamchatka and forms the northern part of the Pacific Ring of Fire. Other volcanoes that have been active during the last few thousand years are located in southeastern Alaska, and in the Wrangell Mountains. Smaller volcanoes are located in the interior, and in western Alaska, as far north as the Seward Peninsula.

Volcanic hazards Western United States

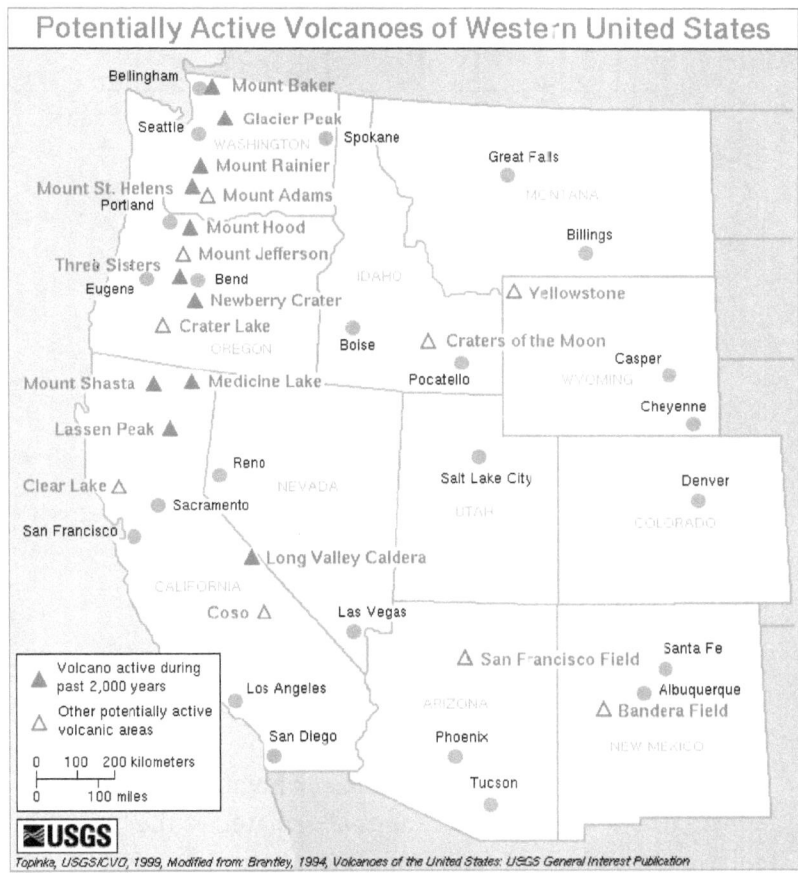

The Cascade Volcanoes (also known as the Cascade Volcanic Arc or the Cascade Arc) are a number of volcanoes in a volcanic arc in western North America, extending from southwestern British Columbia, through Washington and Oregon, to Northern California, a distance of well over 700 mi (1,100 km).

Volcanic hazards – Colombia

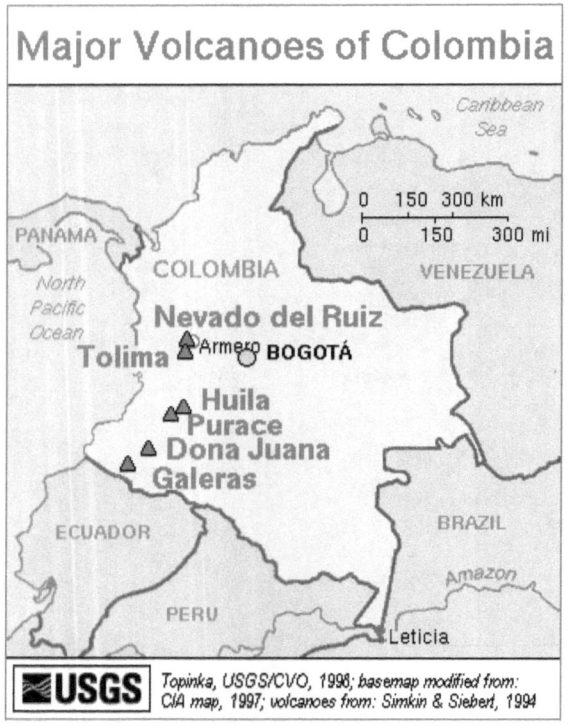

Colombia has a total of 17 volcanoes, of which, 15 are considered active. The volcanoes are related to the subduction zone that runs along the whole of America's western plate margin. Colombia's volcanoes are part of the northern Andes, and lie at the junction of 3 tectonic plates, the Nazca, Caribbean and South American plates. The volcanoes of Colombia include: Romeral | Cerro Bravo | Nevado del Ruiz | Santa Isabel | Nevado del Tolima | Machin | Nevado del Huila | Puracé | Sotará | Petacas | Doña Juana | Galeras | Azufral | Cumbal | Cerro Negro de Mayasquer.

Volcanic hazards – Ecuador

Major Volcanoes in Ecuador

Topinka, USGS/CVO, 2003; basemap modified from:
CIA, 1997; volcanoes from: Simkin & Siebert, 1994

Ecuador has about 26 volcanoes. The volcanoes of Ecuador belong to the Northern Volcanic Zone of the Andes, which is the result of subduction of the Nazca Pacific oceanic plate under the continental plate of South America. In Ecuador, the volcanoes occur on 4 chains. The Galapagos Islands, off the coast of Ecuador, is a volcanic '*hot-spot*' or magma plume. The volcanoes of Ecuador are quite dangerous and some, like Tungurahua, Sangay, and Reventador, frequently erupt. The entire list of volcanoes of Ecuador include: Cerro Negro de Mayasquer | Soche | Chachimbiro | Cuicocha | Imbabura | Mojanda | Pululagua | Cayambe | Reventador | Guagua Pichincha | Atacazo | Chacana | Pan de Azucar | Antisana | Aliso | Sumaco | Iliniza | Cotopaxi | Quilotoa | Cerro Azul | Chimborazo | Tungurahua | Altar | Licto | Sangay.

Volcanic hazards Guatemala

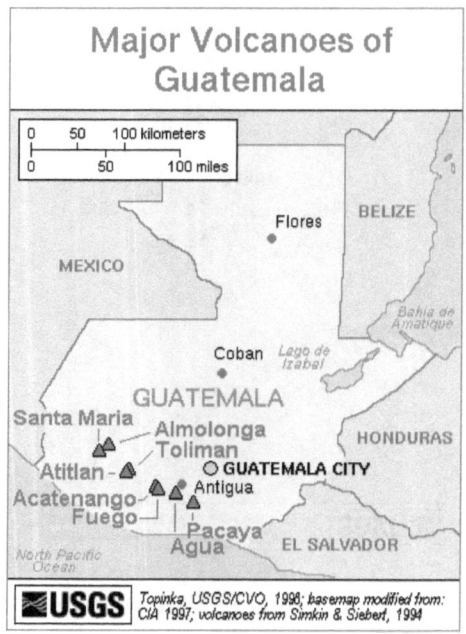

Guatemala has about 33 volcanoes spread throughout its highlands. Guatemala is part of the Caribbean Plate. The Caribbean Plate is an oceanic tectonic plate underlying Central America and the Caribbean Sea, off the north coast of South America. The violent plate is roughly 3.2 million square kilometers (1.2 million square miles) in area; the Caribbean Plate borders the North American Plate, the South American Plate, the Nazca Plate, and the Cocos Plate. These borders are regions of very intense geological activity; including frequent earthquakes, occasional tsunamis, and volcanic eruptions.

Volcanic hazards – Mexico

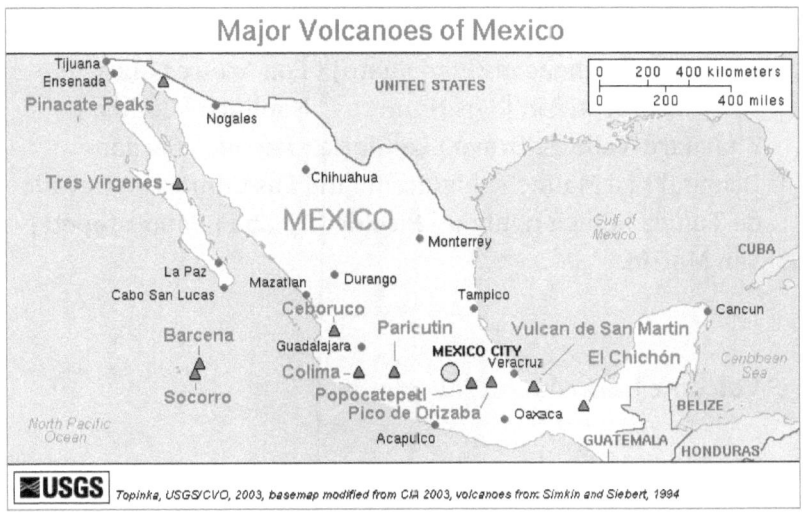

There are about 42 volcanoes located throughout Mexico. Mexico's volcanoes are part of the seismic zone known as the Pacific Ring of Fire, which is formed on the North American continental tectonic plate, under which, the oceanic Pacific and (in the south) the Cocos plates, are being subducted. The Pacific Ocean floor off southern Mexico, however, is being carried northeast by the underlying motion of the Cocos Plate. The most active volcanoes of the country are Popocatepetl, Colima and El Chichón, which had a major eruption in 1982 that cooled the world's climate in the following year. All active volcanoes of Mexico are listed.

Baja California, NW Mexico & Mexican Islands (16 volcanoes): Cerro Prieto | Pinacate | San Quintin | Isla San Luis | Jaraguay | Coronado | Guadaloupe | San Borja |

unnamed | El Aguajito | Tres Virgenes | Isla Tortuga | Punta Pulpito | Comondu-La Purisima | Bárcena | Socorro.

Western & Central Mexico (24 volcanoes): Durango | Sangangüey | Ceboruco | Mascota | Sierra la Primavera | Paricutín (Michoacán-Guanajuato) | Los Azufres | Los Atlixcos | Jocotitlán | Los Humeros | Naolinco | Colima | Zitácuaro-Valle de Bravo | La Gloria | Papayo | Serdán-Oriental | La Malinche | Iztaccíhuatl | Las Cumbres | Nevado de Toluca | Chichinautzin | Pico de Orizaba | Popocatépetl | San Martín.

Volcanic hazards – El Salvador

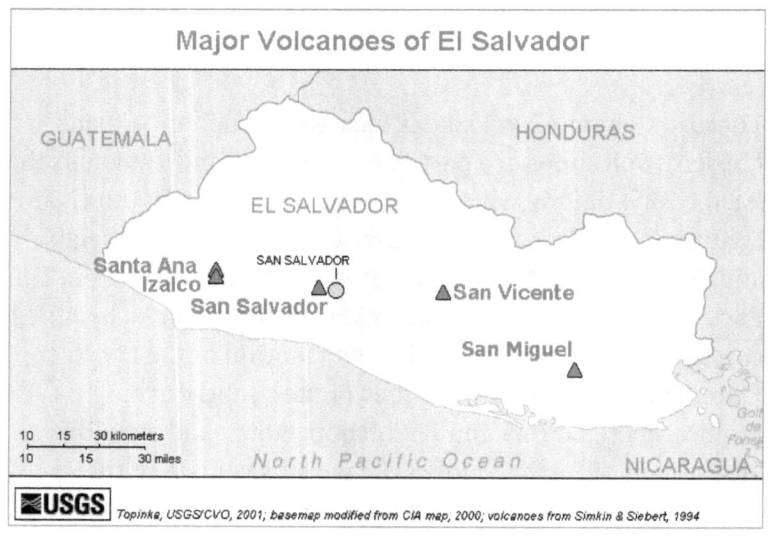

Volcanic hazards - Costa Rica

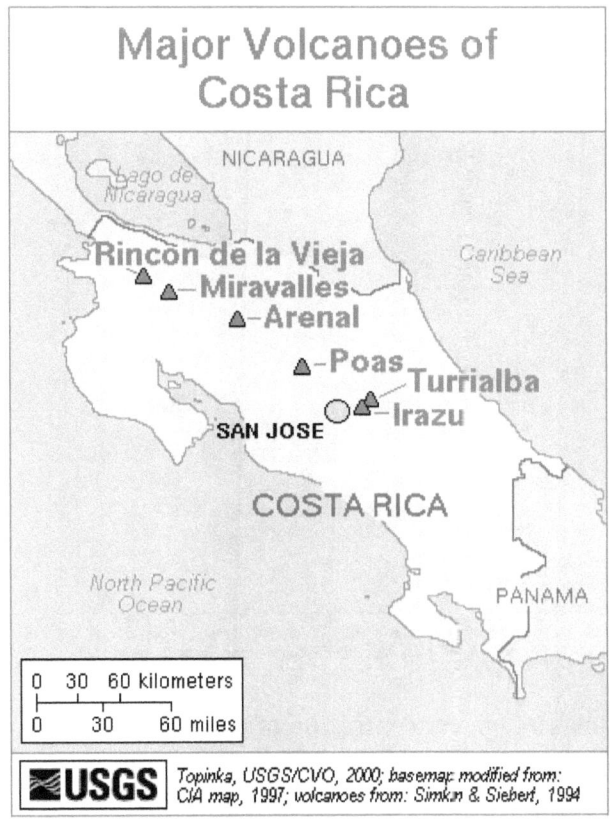

Costa Rica is a small country but it has an impressive chain of volcanoes. The volcanoes are caused by the NE subduction of the Pacific tectonic plate under the Carribean plate. Among Costa Rica's most active volcanoes are: Arenal, Poás and Irazú The list of the countries volcanoes include: Rincón de la Vieja | Arenal | Poas | Turrialba | Irazu.

Volcanic hazards - Iceland

Iceland has a high concentration of active volcanoes, due to the unique geological conditions of its location on the mid-Atlantic Ridge. Iceland sits on a divergent tectonic plate boundary, where it resides over a magma plume. Iceland has 30 active volcanic systems, of which 13 have erupted since the settlement of the country in 874 AD. Of these 30 volcanic Icelandic systems, Grímsvötn is the most active and volatile. Over the past 500 years, Iceland's volcanoes have produced a third of all total global lava output. The most fatal volcanic eruption of Iceland's history was the so-called Skaftáreldar (*fires of Skaftá*) in 1783, which burned voraciously until 1784. The eruption flared up in the crater row, Lakagígar

160

(craters of Laki), southeast of Vatnajökull glacier. The Laki
volcano eruptions killed 25% of the population of Iceland,
and an estimated 7 million people worldwide.

Volcanic hazards – Italy

Volcanic hazards Ethiopia, Eritrea, and Djibouti

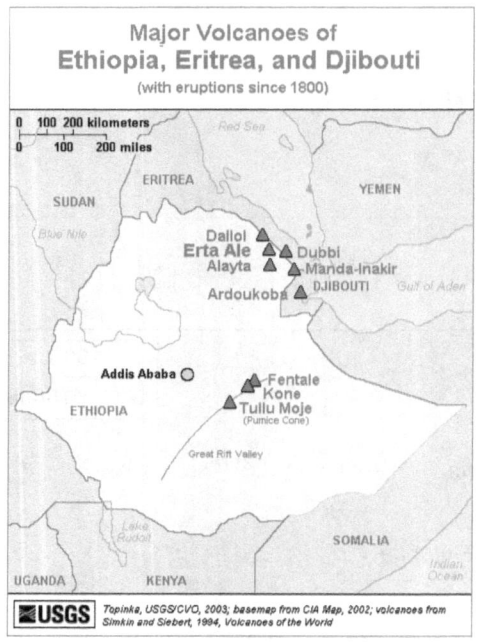

The East African Rift Zone includes a number of active, as well as, dormant volcanoes. Some of these include: Mount Kilimanjaro, Mount Kenya, Mount Longonot, Menengai Crater, Mount Karisimbi, Mount Nyiragongo, Mount Meru, and Mount Elgon, as well as the Crater Highlands in Tanzania. The Ol Doinyo Lengai volcano remains active, and is currently the only natrocarbonatite volcano in the world. Erta Ale is a continuously active basaltic shield volcano in the Afar Region of northeastern Ethiopia. The Mount Nabro volcano in Eritrea erupted for the first time in recorded history in 2011. Eritrea was rocked by a swarm of 5.0 + magnitude tremors preceding the volcanic eruption.

Volcanic hazards – Chile

Major Volcanoes in Chile

Chile has a density of volcanoes, second only to that of Indonesia. Volcanism in Chile, as well as in other parts of the world, is also associated with several natural hazards such as: lahars, earthquakes, pyroclastic flows, toxic gases, and ash. Volcanoes in South America generally erupt longer and have denser volcanic ash emissions. Continental Chile has a high concentration of active volcanoes, due to its location along the Peru-Chile Trench, a subduction zone, where the Nazca and Antarctic Plates are driven beneath the South

American Plate. Chile has been subjected to volcanism since at least the late Paleozoic era, when subduction along the western margin of South America began. Easter Island, Juan Fernández Islands, and other oceanic islands of Chile, are extinct volcanoes created by hotspots. Chile has about 500 volcanoes considered active, 60 of which have had recorded eruptions in the last 450 years.

Volcanic hazards – Caribbean

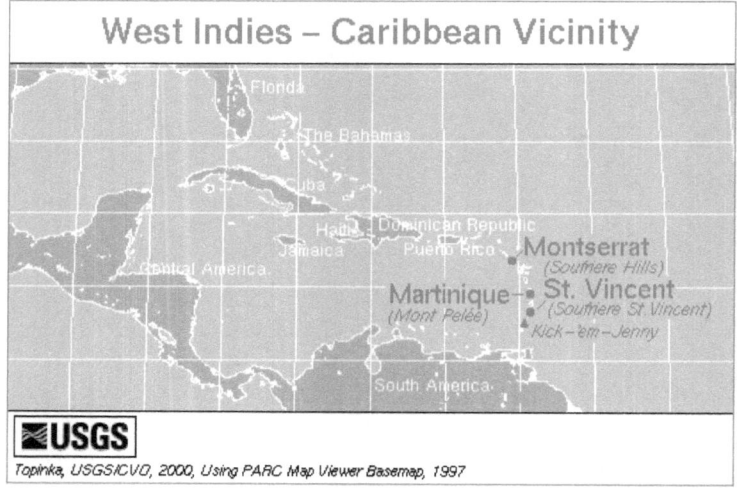

Topinka, USGS/CVO, 2000, Using PARC Map Viewer Basemap, 1997

There are about 20 volcanoes in the Caribbean. The Caribbean plate is responsible for the region's turbulent geology. The northern boundary, with the North American plate is a transform, or strike-slip. The eastern boundary is a subduction zone. The southern boundary is complex and is partly the result of transform faulting, thrust faulting, and subduction.

Volcanic hazards – Japan

Major Volcanoes of Japan

Volcanic hazards – New Zealand

Volcanic hazards – Philippines

Volcanic hazards – Papua New Guinea

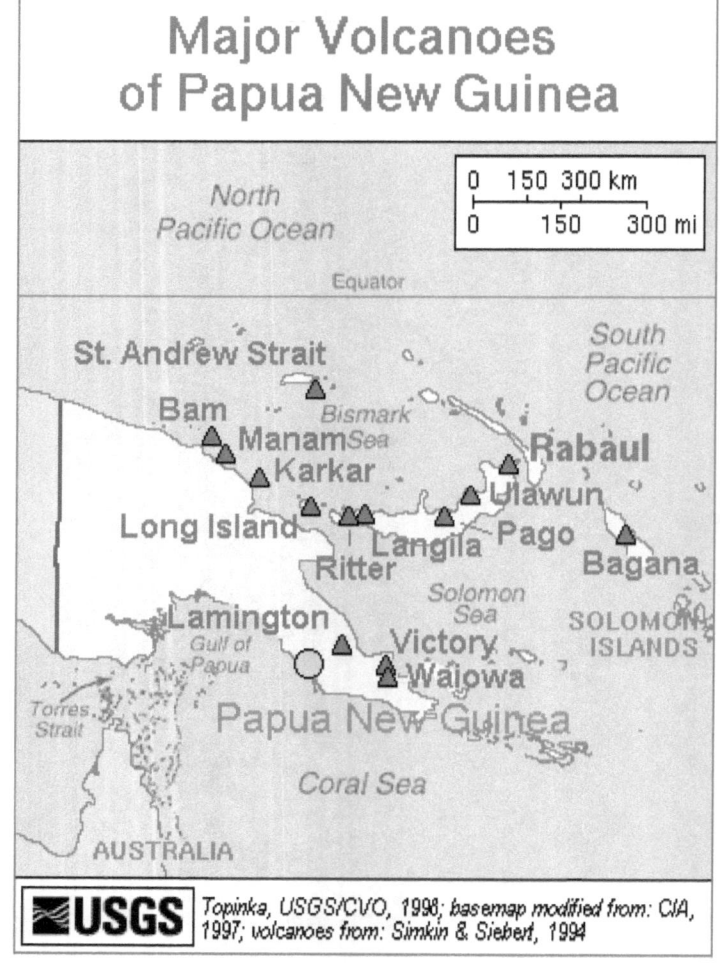

Volcanic hazards – Vanuatu

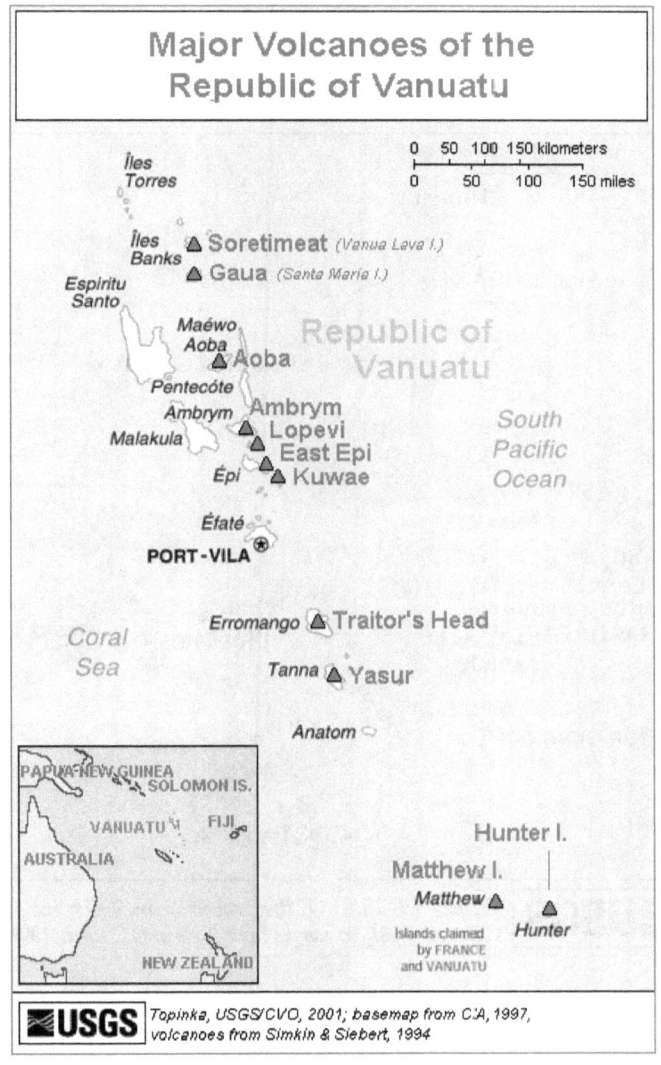

Major Volcanoes of the Republic of Vanuatu

Volcanic hazards – Nicaragua

Volcanic hazards – Tanzania

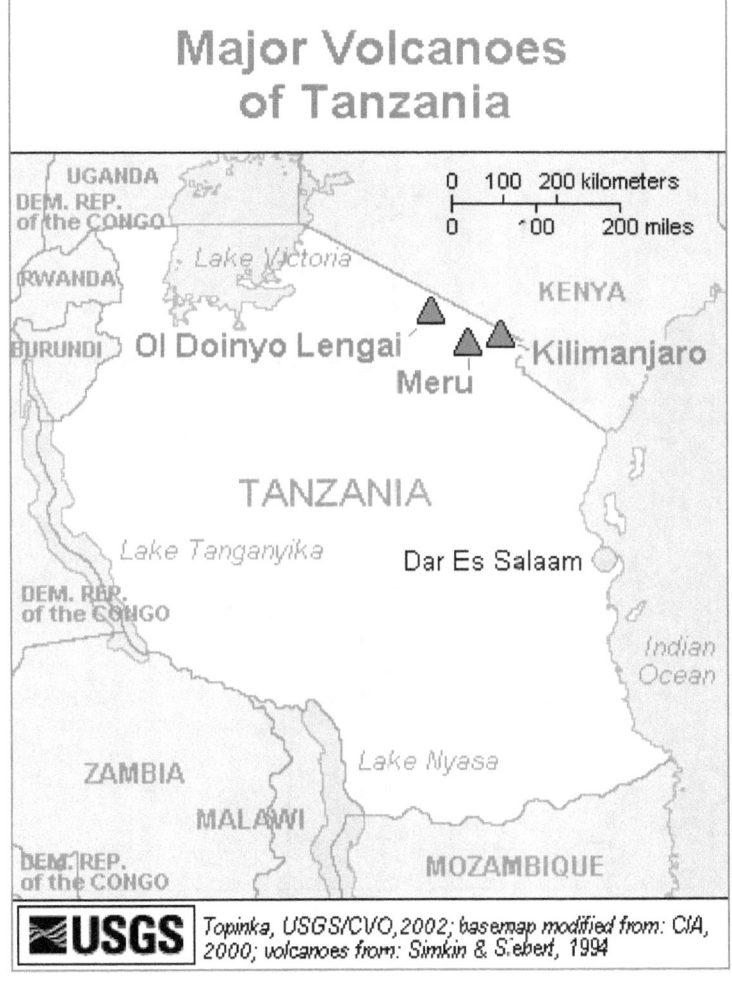

Volcanic hazards – Democratic Republic of Congo

East Africa Rift Map

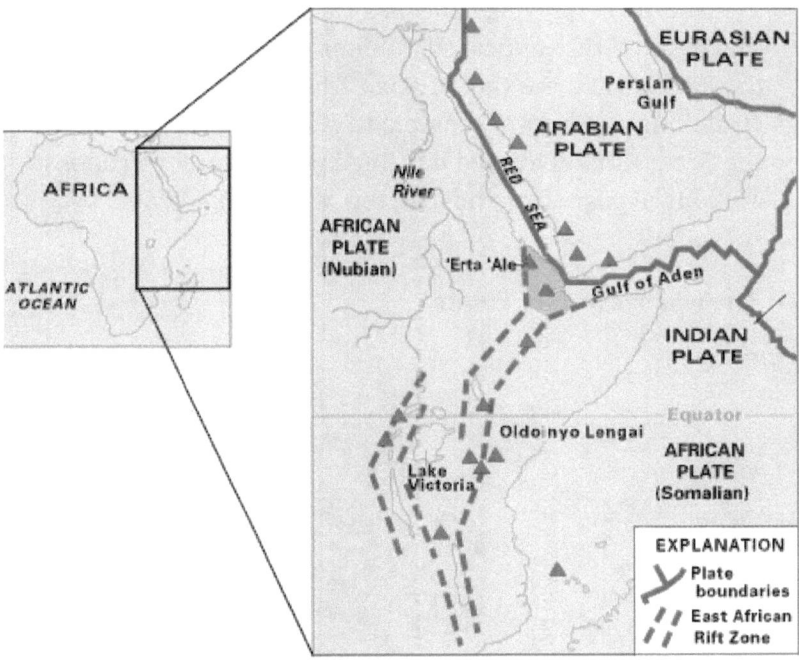

The Great Rift Valley is an active continental rift zone in eastern Africa that appears to be a developing divergent tectonic plate boundary. The eastern portion of the continent of Africa is actually rifting in two. The rift is a narrow zone, where the African Plate is in the process of splitting into two new tectonic plates, the Somali Plate and the Nubian Plate, which are subplates or protoplates. The future look of this region is uncertain. The tearing of the African continent, however, is not. An article in *Spiegel* magazine summed up the tremendous change taking place on the East Africa continent: "The earth is in upheaval in northeastern Africa, and the region is changing quickly. The desert floor is quaking and splitting open, volcanoes are boiling over, and seawaters are encroaching upon the land. Africa, researchers are certain, is splitting apart at a rate rarely seen in geology. The first fracture appeared millions of years ago, resulting in the Red Sea and the Gulf of Aden. The second fracture, stretching south from Ethiopia to Mozambique, is known as the Great Rift Valley, and it is lined with several volcanoes. Millions of years from now, it, too, will be filled with seawater." [1]

Earthchanges Stress Points

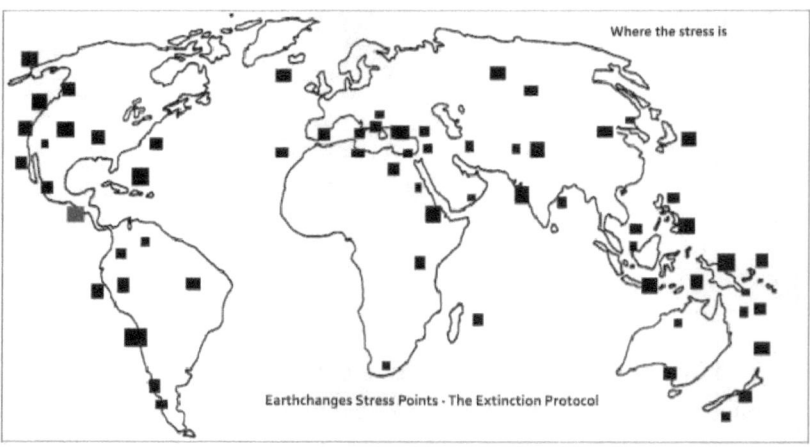

Earthchanges Stress Points · The Extinction Protocol

As the planet experiences an inconsolable thermal anomaly, and the planet's magnetic field continues to deteriorate in dexterity, due to thermal gradient changes in the Mantle Core Boundary (MCB), the planet will dissipate more heat through catastrophism involving: earthquakes, volcanism, mantle plume activity, sea-floor spreading, and continental rifting. The squares on the map above represent geological stress points on the globe, where catastrophic risk is high.

Tsunami – the rage of the ocean

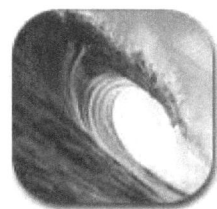 A tsunami is a series of ocean waves generated by sudden displacements in the sea floor from earthquakes, landslides, or volcanic activity. Tsunamis can also be generated by glacier calving (sudden breaking and collapse of walls of ice), and meteor impacts. In the deep ocean, the tsunami wave may only be a few inches high. The tsunami wave may come gently ashore or it may increase in height to become a fast moving wall of turbulent water several meters high. Although a tsunami cannot be prevented, the impact of a tsunami can be mitigated through community preparedness, timely warnings, and effective evacuation response.

Tsunami waves do not resemble normal sea waves because their wavelength is considered far longer. Instead of a breaking wave, a tsunami may instead initially resemble a rapidly rising tide. Tsunamis are often referred to as tidal waves, for this reason. Tsunamis typically consist of a series of waves with periods ranging from minutes to hours. These tidal waves or tsunamis arrive in a so-called *"wave train,"* sometimes growing in height as they fan out from the point of origin. Wave heights of tens of meters can be generated by large events. Although the impact of tsunamis is limited to coastal areas, their destructive power can be enormous, and can affect entire ocean basins. The 2004 Indian Ocean tsunami was among the deadliest natural disasters in human history, resulting in 230,000 deaths in 14 countries, bordering the Indian Ocean. The largest tsunami ever recorded, occurred in Alaska. On July 9, 1958, an earthquake along the Fairweather Fault in the Alaska Panhandle loosened about 40 million cubic yards (30.6 million cubic meters) of rock high above the northeastern shore of Lituya Bay. This mass of rock plunged from an altitude of 3,000 feet (914 meters) into the waters of Gilbert Inlet. The avalanche generated tsunami waves 1,720 feet (524 meters) high. The volume of water was so high, and the tidal wave was so powerful, that it completely stripped mountainsides of all trees and vegetation.

Tsunami risk regions of the world

U.S. tsunami risks: Alaska, NW, SE, East coast, and Lake Tahoe

If you live along the coastal region of one of the high-risk zones highlighted on the above map, you should always be prepared for the likelihood of a tsunami. Most densely populated coastal enclaves in tsunami zones have tsunami sirens. In Japan, alerts are sent to coastal residents by mobile phones, via an elaborate text messaging system. If you are at work in a high-rise building or vacationing in a resort when a large earthquake strikes under the sea-floor, move immediately to higher ground. Many tsunamis are generated when megathrust earthquakes rupture the sea-floor.

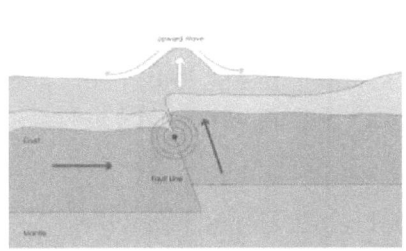

Megathrust earthquakes are some of the most powerful seismic forces of nature. They occur in subduction zones, when one tectonic plate is shoved under another. They are believed to be the only known types of tectonic activity capable of producing 9.0 magnitude earthquakes or higher. During the rupture, one side of the fault is pushed upwards relative to the other. This type of fault movement is known as a thrust. In these events, huge volumes of ocean water are suddenly displaced, and a tsunami wave is the result.

The Defense

HAZARD THREAT

Strategy: Surviving a tsunami requires preparation, and a quick response time in the event of a disaster. If you have a mobile phone, download an earthquake app on your phone or mobile device. Set alerts on the app that will prompt you when a disaster strikes. Most earthquake apps will even alert you with the distance you are from the earthquake's epicenter by the GPS.

- Have an emergency survival kit that's sufficient to get you through at least three days of isolation until help arrives. It should contain emergency items, a flashlight, water, non-perishable food, thermal blankets, a first-aid kit, a laser pointer, a surgical mask, a compass, and insect repellent.

- Move immediately to higher ground, if you are in a low-lying coastal area. If you have a limited amount of time to get to safety, climb to the highest point of a building or take shelter on the roof of a very sturdy building. Remember, every second you delay is a second off your life because tsunami waters sweep inland very fast. A typical 300 ft, or 100 meter high wave can travel at speeds of up to 800 kilometers per hour (500 mph). You can't outrun it, once it's in visual range.

- Heed natural warnings. Frantic animal behavior before or after an earthquake in a coastal area, is a pretty good indicator something is amiss. A rapid rise and fall in coastal waters or the sea suddenly receding (draws back), leaving bare sand, are all major warning signs that there is about to be a sudden surge of water inland.

- Do not try to survive a tsunami by trying to swim through it with a life preserver. The waves carry debris, rocks, boulders, houses, ships, and even cars. Even if you miraculously survive the trauma of the debris in the wave surge, you could still be swept back out to sea when the tidal wave recedes.

- Once the tsunami has subsided, there will be debris, destroyed buildings, and broken infrastructure. There may also be dead bodies washed inland. Fresh water and food supplies will likely be unavailable. The potential for disease, post-traumatic stress disorder, grief, starvation, and injuries could make the post-tsunami period nearly as perilous as the disaster itself. Be prepared for numerous hardships.

The art of the communiqué

Depending on the distress of your situation or national emergency, you may need to communicate with emergency services, government officials, family or associates, or you may need to have minimum communication if you and your party have been separated during a crisis event in a foreign country. In which case, you might want to invoke what's known as the *Moscow Rules* of survival. (*page 183*)

Emergency Services

Emergency

Phone numbers: The following dial codes listed below will put you in contact with emergency services officials across the world depending on the country you're in at the time of any incident or emergency.

Argentina – 101   Australia – 000

Bolivia – 110   Brazil – 190

Canada – 911   Caribbean – 999   Chile – 133

China – 110   Colombia – 156   Central America – 110

Egypt – 122   Europe – 112

Greenland – 112

Hong Kong - 999

Israel – 100   Iran – 110   Indonesia – 110

Italy – 112   India - 102

Japan – 110

Kuwait – 112

Mexico – 066   Middle East - 999

New Zealand – 111

Pakistan – 15

Peru – 105

Russia – 112

Singapore – 999   South Korea and Syria – 112

Saudi Arabia - 999   Sri Lanka – 119   South Africa - 10177

Taiwan – 110   Turkey – 155   Thailand – 191

Vatican – 113   Venezuela – 171   Vietnam – 113

U.S. – 911   United Kingdom – 999

United States: Other Emergency Services

CHEMTREC (Chemical Transportation Emergency Center), a 24-hour emergency response communications service, for immediate information about a chemical or to seek assistance from a manufacturer, 800-424-9300 (toll free US, CA, US Virgin Islands), 703-527-3887 for calls originating elsewhere (collect calls are accepted).

CHEM-TEL, INC., a 24-hour emergency response communications service, 800-255-3924 (toll free US, CA, US Virgin Islands), 813-248-0585 for calls originating elsewhere (collect calls are accepted).

INFOTRAC, a 24-hour emergency response communications service, 800-535-5053 (toll free US, CA, US Virgin Islands), 352-323-3500 for calls originating elsewhere (collect calls are accepted).

3E COMPANY, a 24-hour emergency response communications service, 800-451-8346 (toll free US, CA, US Virgin Islands), 760-602-8703 for calls originating elsewhere (collect calls are accepted).

The emergency response information services shown above have requested to be listed as providers of emergency response information and have agreed to provide emergency response information to all callers. They maintain periodically updated lists of state and Federal radiation authorities who provide information and technical assistance on handling incidents involving radioactive materials.

NATIONAL RESPONSE CENTER (NRC) 800-424-8802 (toll free US, Canada, US Virgin Islands), 202-267-2675 in the District of Columbia.

The NRC, which is operated by the US Coast Guard, receives reports required when dangerous goods and hazardous substances are spilled. After receiving notification of an incident, the NRC will immediately notify the appropriate

Federal On-Scene Coordinator and concerned Federal agencies. Federal law requires that anyone who releases into the environment a reportable quantity of a hazardous substance (including oil when water is, or may be affected) or a material identified as a marine pollutant must **immediately** notify the NRC. When in doubt as to whether the amount released equals the required reporting levels for these materials, the NRC should be notified.

MILITARY SHIPMENTS

For assistance at incidents involving materials being shipped by, for, or to the Department of Defense (DOD), call one of the following numbers (24 hours): 703-697-0218 (call collect) (US Army Operations Center) For explosives/ammunition incidents, please call 800-851-8061 (toll-free in the US)(Defense Logistics Agency) For all other dangerous goods incidents.

The above numbers are for **EMERGENCIES** only.

Mexico:

SETIQ (Emergency Transportation System for the Chemical Industry), a service of the Association of Chemical Industries (ANIQ) 01-800-00-214-00 in the Mexican Republic; for calls originating in Mexico City and the Metropolitan Area 5559-1588. For calls originating elsewhere, call dial +52-55-5559-1588

CECOM (the National Center for Communications of the Civil Protection Agency) 01-800-00-413-00 in the Mexican Republic; for calls originating in Mexico City and the Metropolitan Area 5550-1496, 5550-1552, 5550-1485 or 5550-4885. For calls originating elsewhere, call 0-11-52-5-550-1496, or 0-11-52-5-550-1552, or 0-11-52-5-550-1485, or 0-11-52-5-550-4885.

Brazil:

PRÓ-QUÍMICA 0-800-118270 (Toll-free in Brazil); +55-11-232-1144 for calls originating elsewhere (collect calls are accepted).

The Moscow Rules

The Moscow Rules is the name for a set of rules developed during the Cold War that were to be used by spies and covert operatives working in Moscow, Russia. The rules are associated with Moscow because the city developed a reputation, during the Cold War era, of being a particularly harsh locale for clandestine operatives, who were exposed by enemy agents. Many consider the list to be a no-nonsense safety protocol for surviving in an environment where you are either an outsider, or under surveillance. You may be visiting a country which could become a hostile environment if a terrorist act or a war broke out.

- Assume nothing.
- Never go against your gut.
- Everyone is potentially under opposition control.
- Don't look back; you are never completely alone.
- Go with the flow, blend in.
- Vary your pattern and stay within your cover.
- Lull them into a sense of complacency.
- Don't harass the opposition.
- Pick the time and place for action.

- Keep your options open.
- Never make contact with a friendly party when you suspect you are under surveillance.
- Consider you new environment hostile terrain if your identity is compromised.
- Get off the grid and go zero-tech.

Morse code

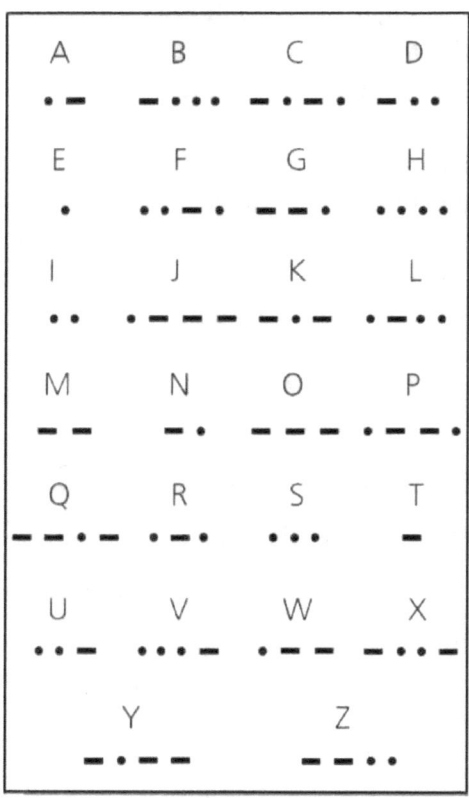

Distress signals

Distress - in the mountains

CARRY a WHISTLE, you give help and get help with one.

In Europe, the standardised European emergency call number 112 can in principle be used anywhere. Mobile phones can also be used, but one must understand that mobile phones services may not always be accessed in mountainous regions.

International Distress signal (to be used in emergency only)
Six blasts on a whistle, mirroir (and flashes on a torch or camera flashes after dark) spaced evenly for a minute, followed by a minutes pause. Repeat until an answer is received.

The response is three signals per minute followed by a minutes pause.

Basic signals to communicate with a helicopter.

Helped needed: Raise both arms above your head to form ' V'.

All OK: Raise one arm above your head and lower the the arm to form an oblique line with your arms.

Making a fire

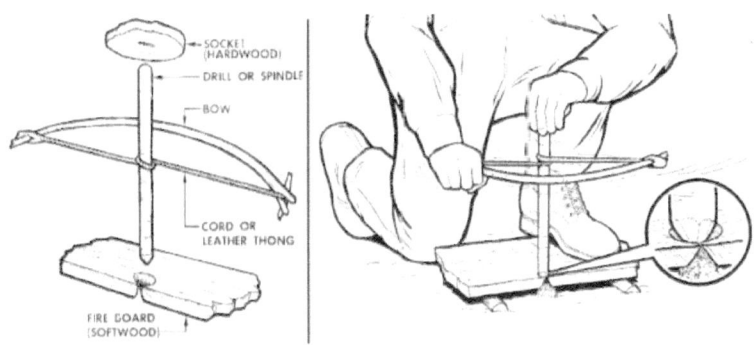

185

Ground-Air Emergency Code

Require doctor—
serious injuries.

Require medical
supplies.

Unable to proceed.

Require food
and water.

Require firearms
and ammunition.

Indicate direction
to proceed.

Am proceeding
in this direction.

Will attempt
to take off.

Aircraft badly
damaged.

Phonetic alphabet

Phonetic Alphabet

A - alpha	N - november
B - bravo	O - oscar
C - charlie	P - papa
D - delta	Q - quebec
E - echo	R - romeo
F - foxtrot	S - sierra
G - golf	T - tango
H - hotel	U - uniform
I - india	V - victor
J - juliet	W - wiskey
K - kilo	X - x-ray
L - lima	Y - yankee
M - mike	Z - zulu

Quick Medical Reference

Although there are well over 100 antibiotics, the majority come from only a few types of drugs. These are the main classes of antibiotics.

Penicillins such as penicillin and amoxicillin
Cephalosporins such as cephalexin (Keflex)
Macrolides such as erythromycin (E-Mycin), clarithromycin (Biaxin), and azithromycin (Zithromax)
Fluoroquinolones such as ciprofloxacin (Cipro), levofloxacin (Levaquin), and ofloxacin (Floxin)
Sulfonamides such as co-trimoxazole (Bactrim) and trimethoprim (Proloprim)
Tetracyclines such as tetracycline (Sumycin, Panmycin) and doxycycline (Vibramycin)
Aminoglycosides such as gentamicin (Garamycin) and tobramycin (Tobrex)

Most antibiotics have 2 names, the trade or brand name, created by the drug company that manufactures the drug, and a generic name, based on the antibiotic's chemical structure or chemical class. Trade names such as Keflex and Zithromax are capitalized. Generics such as cephalexin and azithromycin are not capitalized.

Each antibiotic is effective only for certain types of infections, and your doctor is best able to compare your needs with the available medicines. Also, a person may have allergies that eliminate a class of antibiotic from consideration, such as a penicillin allergy preventing your doctor from prescribing amoxicillin.

In most cases of antibiotic use, a doctor must choose an antibiotic based on the most likely cause of the infection. For example, if you have an earache, the doctor knows what kinds of bacteria cause most ear infections. He or she will choose the antibiotic that best combats those kinds of bacteria. In another example, a few bacteria cause about 90% of pneumonias in previously healthy people. If you are diagnosed with pneumonia, the doctor will choose an antibiotic that will kill these bacteria.

Risk mitigation statistical factoid

- Communicable diseases kill about 14 million people a year
- About 60 percent of all human diseases, and 75 percent of all emerging infectious diseases, are zoonotic (originates from animals). Most human infections with zoonoses come from livestock, including: pigs, chickens, cattle, goats, sheep and camels. Out of 56 zoonotic diseases studied, the researchers found 13 that were most important in terms of their impact on human deaths. They are, in descending order: zoonotic gastrointestinal disease; leptospirosis; cysticercosis; zoonotic tuberculosis (TB); rabies; leishmaniasis (caused by a bite from certain sandflies); brucellosis (a bacterial disease that mainly infects livestock); echinococcosis; toxoplasmosis; Q fever; zoonotic trypanosomiasis (sleeping sickness), hepatitis E; and anthrax
- The U.S. averages 1,200 tornadoes per year
- The highest number of tornadoes per year, occurs in the Netherlands
- Lightning has a mortality rate of between 10 and 30%

- 80% of victims of lightning strikes sustain long-term health issues
- Lightning is the second most common cause of weather related fatalities
- The odds of you being hit by a lighting strike is 1/1,000,000
- As little as 2 feet (0.61 m) of water is enough to carry away most SUV-sized vehicles. The U.S. National Weather Service reported in 2005 that, using a national 30-year average, more people die yearly in floods, 127 on average, than by lightning (73), tornadoes (65), or hurricanes (16)
- 70% of the deaths that take place during a blizzard, happen to people who are traveling during a winter storm
- 33% of avalanche victims are killed by trauma, not the snow
- If an avalanche victim survives the trauma, they have a 90% chance of survival, provided they can be rescued in 30 minutes or less.
- 500,000 earthquakes occur in the world each year
- 100,000 earthquakes occur each year that are large enough to be felt
- 90% of all the earthquakes on the planet, take place in the Pacific Ring of Fire
- 81% of the world's largest earthquakes take place in the Pacific Ring of Fire
- Earthquakes kill 10,000 people a year, on average
- Your chances of dying in an earthquake are about 1 in 131,000
- 75% of all earthquake fatalities result from the structural collapse of buildings

- Your odds of being killed in a tsunami anywhere in the world are 1 in 50,000; in the U.S., 1 in 500,000
- 14% of all males that die in the world are killed by an act of violence
- 7% of all women that die in the world are killed by an act of violence
- The chances of you being killed by an asteroid impact is 1 in 500,000
- In 2012, NASA said 4,700 Near Earth asteroids pose a threat to Earth
- For people over 44, the leading cause of death in the U.S. is injury
- For people over 65, the leading cause of death in the U.S. is heart attack
- Your chances of dying from cancer are 1 in 7
- Your chances of dying from a stroke are 1 in 23

Bibliography

Manufactured threats, biological, chemical

1. Iodine for Radiation Exposure: Practical Solutions You Need to Know, Natural News, March 16, 2011, http://www.naturalnews.com/031715_iodine_radiation.html#ixzz1vijzZiuh
2. Potassium Iodine KI, Centers for Disease Control and Prevention, Emergency Preparedness and Response, http://www.bt.cdc.gov/radiation/ki.asp

Atmospheric forces of Nature

1. Tornado basics, NOAA, http://www.nssl.noaa.gov/primer/tornado/tor_basics.html

Earthquakes and seismic hazards

1. Probability of contamination from severe nuclear reactor accidents is higher than expected, Physics.org, May 22, 2012, http://phys.org/news/2012-05-probability-contamination-severe-nuclear-reactor.html

2. Europe starting to dive under Africa? National Geographic, April 19, 2011, http://news.nationalgeographic.com/news/2011/04/110419-europe-africa-mediterranean-earthquake-risk-increasing-earth-science/

Volcanic hazards

1. Violent Seismic Activity Tearing Africa in Two, January 20, 2011, Spiegel

Special thanks

The USGS for maps

NOAA

The Extinction Protocol Readers

About the Author

Alvin Conway is an author, poet, journalist, science advisor, videographer, and artist. He has lectured extensively on the subjects of historical movements in art and literature, physics and geology, as well as the meaning of symbolism and iconography in ancient and contemporary myth, history, religion and psychology. He is co-host of the popular Earth changes on-air program, *The Extinction Protocol Radio.* He is also the author of *The Extinction Protocol: 2012 and beyond,* an in-depth study volume on the science and mythology behind Earth changes, extinctions, and the geological transition of epochs in terrestrial planetary history. *The 7th Protocol* is a detailed study of astrophysical catastrophism and the geological processes which destroy planets. His literary poetic collection includes: *Ariel and the Fountain of Seven Graces, Sinfonia 9: the Second Movement, Esprit: the Third Movement,* The *Amethyst,* and *Callidora.*

Select books by the author:

The Extinction Protocol
The 7th Protocol
Hazard
Sparkle
Ariel and the Fountain of Seven Graces
Sinfonia 9: The Second Movement
Esprit: The Third Movement
The Amethyst
Callidora
Utopia
The Tipping Point

www.alvinconway.com

The Sparkle Series: The Social Science books

"A revolutionary new way of viewing the relationships between science, wealth, ecology, love and the Bible." –Fringe Science

"A masterpiece of science and spirituality" –NY Beat